COOKING
with *Cornelius*

The CORNING
COOKBOOK

COOKING
with *Cornelius*

The CORNING
COOKBOOK

Cornelius O'Donnell

Random House 🏠 *New York*

Library of Congress Cataloging in Publication Data
O'Donnell, Cornelius.
  Cooking with Cornelius.
  Includes index.
  1. Cookery.   I. Title.   II. Title: The Corning
cookbook.
TX715.O3345   641.5   82–5217
ISBN 0–394–52333–4   AACR2

Manufactured in the United States of America
24689753
First Edition

BOOK DESIGN BY LILLY LANGOTSKY

EDITED BY JERI LABER

Contents

❧Acknowledgments

Do these recipes work? Do they taste as good as they sound? Of course they do, thanks to Corning's Product Appraisal Department (otherwise known as the Test Kitchen). A sincere "well done" to Carol Hacker, Helen Carrell, Dawn Towner and Kathryn Elmer, who spent an entire summer cooking. Thanks, too, to my fellow Corningites who spent that same summer tasting and telling us when we were right *and* when we were wrong (and tasting the revisions). As for the food that was tasted, I have so many friends to thank: San Francisco's Loni Kuhn and Cleveland's Bill Dollard—both inspired cooks and inspiring teachers, and, closer to home, my beloved "corps de cuisine"—Ellen Azorin, Mary Cassetti, Patricia Cusick, Patricia Hangen and Morgan Stebbins, whose ideas fill these pages. Very special thanks to my right- and left-hand associate, Nancy Dorwart, who not only grows beautiful food but knows how to cook it beautifully. George M. Cochran, the photographer, Bryan N. Hyde, the illlustrator, and Helga Scharr Weinrit, the food stylist, made a really valuable contribution to the book's appearance. A deep bow to Bob Murray, Frank Fenno and Alice Allen, whose encouragement and palates never faltered. And, finally, three cheers for my assistant, Kay Smyers, who typed this manuscript. Although she didn't gain a pound through it all, she gained a lot of friends.

COOKING
with *Cornelius*

The CORNING
COOKBOOK

❧Introduction

A few years ago I began writing a column, "Cornelius for Corning," which appears regularly in a number of magazines. It was dedicated to the principle that good cooking need not be complicated or time-consuming—if it's done with a little ingenuity, creativity and good planning.

This cookbook is actually an extension of "Cornelius for Corning." It includes my favorite recipes from the column and many, many more. I think you will be pleased to discover that they're all not only easy but fun.

My "Cornelius for Corning" column has also given me an opportunity to find out what so many American cooks are hungry for. In response to a questionnaire sent to my readers, I have gotten back one overwhelming request: People want recipes, mainly American in flavor, for everyday dishes that they can serve to their families. Very few checked the category "Gourmet Cooking" (whatever *that* is), but many asked for recipes for informal, casual entertaining. Since it's my philosophy that "company" meals shouldn't differ radically from what the family eats, this book aims to meet *both* needs at the same time.

The recipes in this book are for good food, simple food, food that can be assembled easily at the end of an exhausting day. There are dishes here that are, or will instantly become, family favorites, yet with just a little more care in presenting the food, some good dinnerware and linen napkins, the addition of a first course and perhaps some wine, these same "standbys" will make your guests feel like royalty at your table. There are lots of mouth-watering desserts here, too, the kind that will leave everyone—guests and family—asking for more.

As part of my job as spokesperson for Corning's Consumer Products Division, I've traveled all over the country visiting stores and giving demonstrations. These travels have shown me that cooking is "in." Prepackaged, plastic food and the can-opener school of culinary art are "out." Fast foods may be okay for lunch, but most of the time we want our cakes and quiche made from scratch.

Time is the problem—no one has enough of it these days for the kind of leisurely cooking that we can only afford when we're on vacation or for special occasions. I'm always short of time, too, and so most of the recipes I've chosen for this book can be prepared relatively quickly; those that *do* take time will usually reward you with additional meals later on, made from precious leftovers. Meals made from leftovers are often even better than the main event, and there is nothing like the sense of well-being that a "planned second meal" can give a cook.

Menu planning is a personal matter but, in my opinion, absolutely essential if you want to cut down on time and expense. I believe in gearing menus to foods that are readily available in a particular season: They're cheaper, riper and "seem right" when you serve them. I also believe in long-term planning—for three or four days, or even a week at a time. One of the concluding chapters gives a series of weekly menu plans, one for each season of the year, based on the recipes in this book. You may wish to vary them according to your tastes and needs, but the general principle of planning ahead, with paper and pencil, is well worth perfecting and is usually the true secret behind the stellar performances we all admire in our friends who are accomplished home cooks.

Organization is intrinsic to menu planning. It is also the key to relaxation. Begin with an uncluttered kitchen, well equipped with utensils and staple foods that are ready to hand. Banish to the attic or garage those seldom-used gadgets, as well as schoolbooks, old letters, mending, and the general mess that accumulates, especially in a lived-in kitchen. *Read a recipe through several times before you begin to make it, and set out the ingredients you'll need.* The recipes in this book not only list the ingredients first and in the order of use but also give instructions for preparing them prior to cooking—washing, slicing, parboiling, mixing together, whatever. Grease the pans, preheat the oven; clean up as you go along. (If you are lucky enough to have small helpers, these are good jobs for them!) Often you can prepare an entire meal by reusing a few basic utensils over and over again. This is all part of "being organized," and your unruffled appearance at the dinner table, as well as the quality of your food, are the payoff.

The ingredients called for in these recipes, by the way, should all be readily available. Living in Corning, New York, many miles from a major metropolitan area, has had a sobering effect on me: I figure that if *I* can get the stuff, *you* can get it, too. If not, it's easy enough to invent a substitute or even just to leave something out. Don't be a slave to a recipe. Put yourself into it! The important thing is that your food be subtly and well seasoned, and that takes *lots of tasting* and some experience.

The excessive use of salt is discussed almost every day in the media. We Americans are consuming far more salt than our bodies need, and it seems to me, therefore, that it's important to eliminate salt from recipes whenever herbs, spices, garlic, etc., can be used for flavoring, or when salted ingredients like prepared mustard, mayonnaise, broths, canned vegetables, soy sauce and cheeses are already being used.

In this book, though I have often indicated salt, its use is *optional,* or is to be *added to taste.* Of course, those who, like myself, have drastically reduced the amount of salt they take are probably used to the taste of food *without* much salt. Taste, taste, taste while cooking, and vary the spices and herbs to your own palate. (I'm tempted to tell you to take this advice with a grain of salt. There, I've said it!)

Incidently, although we rarely have specified, we recommend that you use *unsalted butter* (or margarine, if you prefer) for all recipes calling for butter in this book. It's better for you and I like the taste much more (just as I prefer butter to margarine—by a wide margin).

Keep expanding your repertoire of seasonings that can dramatically change the taste of foods: soy sauce, sherry, hot peppers and sauces, herbs and spices. That way, you'll never serve boring food or get into a cooking rut!

I guess I'm a frustrated painter, but I truly enjoy figuring out the best way to arrange food on a platter or plate, taking color, shape and design into consideration. Again, it helps if you give it some thought ahead of time, while you're stirring or chopping or browning. But don't get carried away. I remember attending a world-famous cooking class at a seashore location where the *pièce de résistance,* a whole poached salmon, was almost ruined in its sea of green mayonnaise waves as the chef's assistant spent precious time, in a humid 90 degrees, covering the body of the fish with "scales" made from the sheerest rounds of cucumber.

Good cooks must have a sense of adventure and a willingness to experiment with food. To the extent that I have these qualities, I have both my parents to thank. My mother, for example, was known for her sauerbraten, an unusual dish for a woman whose parents had emigrated from Ireland. She did this dish so magnificently that, even today, I refuse to buy any cookbook that offers a sauerbraten recipe calling for gingersnaps for thickening. Only browned flour would do for Genevieve O'Donnell, and I, as a child, spent what seemed like hours over a Dutch oven carefully stirring the flour so that it didn't scorch. Many years later my sister-in-law suggested to Mother that it would be far easier and less risky to brown the flour in a jelly roll pan in the oven (stirring only occasionally). To Mother's credit, she instantly took this advice and made sauerbraten even more often this new simplified way.

My father also took a shine to the kitchen. *His* specialty was baking, for he was the cake eater in the family. No one made a better "from scratch" cake than Father (as he himself readily admitted!). He taught me to have confidence in what I did and never to admit disaster—except to myself. Though I can't say I always abide by this, I try not to be the classic nervous cook who always presents a dish with a built-in excuse, such as "I couldn't find that special ingredient," or "I was interrupted and the sauce burned."

For heaven's sake, let's relax. It's not the end of the world, even when something goes wrong. Let your family and friends enjoy you, one another's company and the wonderful ritual of sharing food around the dinner table.

I hope this book helps you to put together some good, honest meals. And to have fun doing it!

Some Tips to Make Cooking Easier

Tips are little words of wisdom, derived from experience, that make cooking easier, more economical and more gratifying. Each tip, by itself, may not seem earth-shattering, but together they make for organized, efficient cooking and an easier life.

The more I cook, teach and demonstrate, the more tips I develop; my collection would probably fill several volumes. Here are just a few that may help you get your cooking life together.

I. KITCHEN STORAGE AND EQUIPMENT

- Mark the purchase date on staples that you tend to stockpile, so that you can use the oldest first. It takes just a second if you keep markers in a handy place in the kitchen.
- Cover hard cheese with cheesecloth that has been soaked in white wine. It not only keeps cheese soft and fresh, it also adds flavor.
- Freeze fresh herbs (when you have a lot) in foil or plastic bags. When you need some, unwrap enough to snip off the amount you need before reclosing.
- You can dry herbs in minutes between sheets of paper toweling in a microwave oven (yours or a friend's). Consult the instruction book for the specifics.
- One of my favorite ways to preserve the fresh flavor of herbs is to immerse them in a bottle of apple cider vinegar or white wine vinegar. Use tarragon or rosemary or a mixture of fresh herbs. Let the bottle stand for about 2 weeks for the flavor to develop, then use in vinaigrette dressings, lentil or bean soups, as a light sprinkle on cooked fish, or as a perky addition to homemade mayonnaise.
- Store dried herbs and spices where it's dark and cool, well away from the stove and the sun. Always mark the month and year on the bottles when you first open them. After one year, check to see if the flavor and color are still good. If they're not up to snuff, use more than called for and resolve to get a fresh bottle when you next go to the store.
- I recently rearranged my herbs and spices *alphabetically,* using a turntable, as well as narrow spice shelves. What a difference it has made in speeding up cooking and lessening duplication!
- Keep eggs in the refrigerator, small ends down; it keeps the yolks centered. Separated egg yolks will keep 2 to 3 days in cold water in the

refrigerator. Drain before you use. Egg whites will keep for up to a week —without adding water, of course.

- Put an apple, cut in half, into the storage container to keep cakes and baked goods fresh. In hot weather, refrigerate bread.
- Freeze leftovers in individual little dishes that can go in the toaster-oven or microwave. These are great for fast, fast relief of hunger pangs when you're home alone or rushing in and out, and they're so much better than snacking on "junk" foods.
- I freeze fresh berries whole by placing them on cookie sheets in the freezer until they are hard, then storing them in the freezer in plastic bags. (You can do the same with chopped onion or green pepper.)
- Arrange your kitchen cabinets so that the things you use together are stored together. For example, create a baking center by keeping in one cupboard your pie plates, cake dishes, loaf pans, sifter, measuring spoons and cups, rolling pins, and batter bowls. Flours, sugars, cornstarch, baking soda and powder, vanilla, shortening and so on should be kept close by, as well as oils and other liquids used in baking.
- I use the insides of my kitchen cabinet doors. Inside my baking center cabinet, for example, I've taped recipes for my favorite piecrusts and cakes, inserted into plastic sleeves for protection. That way I never have to search through cookbooks—or use my sometimes faulty memory. Tape up your favorite salad dressing, pasta and pancake recipes—anything you make time and time again.
- Do an inventory of your pots, pans, pie plates, cake pans, casseroles and the like, listing the sizes in each category in descending order. Keep the list up-to-date as you acquire new things. Tape it inside a kitchen cabinet, near your cookbook shelf (or planning desk, if you are lucky enough to have one). Then, when a recipe calls for a certain size pot or pan, you'll be able to check and see if you have it *before* you start cooking.
- Keep a pitcher or container full of wooden stirring spoons and spatulas by the stove. It's more than just a decoration; it's so handy.

II. PLANNING AND SHOPPING

- Plan your meals as you would your wardrobe. What goes with what? What are the extras? What can you use from one meal to form the basis for another later in the week?
- Never buy a cookbook for its pretty pictures or short, easy-looking recipes. Take a few moments to *read* several recipes. Check the index for some of your own favorites, then compare those recipes with recipes you already know.

- When you're trying a new recipe, read it through thoroughly before going to the market; there might be a separate sauce suggested—or a garnish or a side dish—that's *not* in the ingredient list.
- I always write in my cookbooks—in pencil, of course. I usually follow a new recipe as it is written the first time around, then indicate on the recipe where I intend to change it the next time I use it. On favorite recipes, I also jot down the exact pan or serving piece I used. This saves a lot of time when I use the recipe again. (If I don't like the recipe at all, I cross it out or mark "don't use.")
- Do you keep track of what you serve at dinner parties? I use an inexpensive steno pad, which works just fine for me. I list the date of the party, who was there, the menu and the source of the recipes. This keeps me from an unconscious inclination to repeat myself with the same friends, which is especially apt to happen when a dish was particularly successful in the past.
- Make a shopping list and stick to it. This is a general rule that's meant to be broken, for an occasional flight of fancy makes living worthwhile. Always be flexible when it comes to fresh vegetables, buying the freshest and working them into your meal plans.
- Always keep on hand such instant salad makers as canned chick peas, cannellini beans and kidney beans; canned sauerkraut, artichoke hearts and beets; quick-cooking lentils; rice (never instant) and the like. They can be cooked up quickly, or just drained if they are already cooked, and they make a perfect base for salads. Unusual pastas, such as fusilli, small shells, bows, ziti and rigatoni are also great for salads. Toss with vinaigrette dressing and serve on lettuce leaves for unexpected—or expected—company. Canned or roasted red pimientos as well as all kinds of olives also do wonders in dressing up a salad.
- Some things you won't find in this book, because I refuse to use them: dried parsley (green sawdust to me); onion flakes; garlic chips; onion, garlic and celery salt; canned or bottled grated cheese (yellow sawdust); bottled lemon juice. In each of these cases the real thing is usually readily available and easy to prepare.
- Try to shop in the same one or two markets where you know the store layout. This makes for speedy "in and out" visits, which make up in time for the money you might save by "bargain hunting."
- Make friends with the store manager, the butcher and the produce manager; learn their names and use them when you see them. Be sure they know yours. Even in the larger stores, personal attention is possible. Once they know you, you can plan your shopping by phone and even have meat trimmed, cut and waiting for you.

- Do watch for "specials" and stock up on the things you always need: paper towels, foil, plastic wrap, canned broth, unsalted butter (freeze it), coffee beans (freeze them), flour, sugar, and the like. My peace of mind comes from having a case of toilet tissue, lots of dishwasher and laundry detergent and a good supply of light bulbs in the house—then I can concentrate on the more perishable things of life, like a good meal!
- Less is more: The smallest zucchini, yellow squash, green beans, carrots, eggplant, sprouts, cucumbers and green onions usually have the best flavor. (An exception is asparagus: Very thin stalks do not have the tenderness of medium stalks.)
- Do not store winter squashes (acorn or butternut) in the fridge. *Always* refrigerate apples, in the crisper if there's room.

III. COOKING

- When I'm entertaining a large group and I'm not sure how much salad they'll consume, I generally pass the oil and vinegar separately (sometimes adding separate dishes of grated cheese, chopped onion, chopped herbs or crumbled bacon). If I have leftover salad tossed with dressing, I put it in the food processor the next day with some canned Italian plum tomatoes and their liquid, and maybe some tomato juice. I add a lot of peppy seasoning, chill it and serve it as a type of gazpacho, adding croutons and chopped fresh cucumbers, peppers and green onions.
- When using carrots for a snack, I cut them on the bias in long, thin "tongue depressor"-shaped slices. I think they have more flavor that way. The sweetest dish of all is freshly made, thinly shredded carrots, served in a bowl and eaten like popcorn. And a food processor makes it so-o-o easy.
- A favorite hors d'oeuvre at my house is young green beans, briefly boiled (or microwaved), then plunged into cold water for 1 second (to stop the cooking). Sprinkle *lightly* with coarse salt and serve, still warm—a whole new taste treat!
- Always have a couple of hard-cooked eggs in the fridge. Mark them with an *H,* using a pencil or a crayon. They're handy for garnishes on vegetables and salads, either sliced in rounds or chopped fine, sometimes with whites and yolks separated.
- If you've purchased a less-than-tender cut of meat that you plan to freeze and marinate sometime in the future, why not freeze it *in* the marinade? Later, as you defrost the meat, the marinade can go right to work!
- Anchovies are a great garnish in salads, salad dressings and hot and cold dishes. If they seem too strong-tasting, soak them for 15 minutes in milk,

then press out the excess liquid before using. You won't need salt in the salad.

- Keep a bagful of odds and ends of vegetables, outside leaves of lettuce, celery leaves and so forth in the freezer or in the fridge to use when making soup stock. I often keep pan drippings, leftover gravy, even the water in which my vegetables were cooked—I feel so self-righteous every time I use things that I once used to toss away!

- Here's a tip that will help you get the most out of those beautiful barbecue coals when you are cooking outdoors: Cook extra steaks, burgers or chicken, wrap them well and freeze them. Reheat the food in your microwave oven, if you're lucky enough to have one. You'll swear it's just come off the coals, and look at the time and energy you'll save!

- Here's a real lifesaver when you are putting together a big dinner party: Cook your fresh vegetables hours ahead and plunge them into cold water when they are *just* barely cooked. Drain and wrap them and keep them in the refrigerator. Before serving, reheat them in the water until just warmed, or drain them and sauté them in a little butter.

- To enhance the flavor of dried herbs, soak them for a few minutes in a little lemon juice and warm water (half and half) before adding them to other ingredients.

- To perk up squash, peas or beans, try adding one or more of the following: bits of chopped ham or crisp bacon; finely chopped, sautéed onions, green onions or shallots; chopped red pimiento or roasted peppers; lightly sautéed sliced mushrooms; finely diced raw celery; finely shredded raw carrots.

- Cheese will grate easily when it's chilled. But, for the best flavor, let it come to room temperature before eating.

- To vary the look and taste of boiled new potatoes, toss them with a little melted butter, combined with any of the following: curry powder, caraway seeds, chopped green olives, capers, chopped walnuts, chives or parsley. Try also a mixture of chopped fresh parsley, dill and mint—it's fabulous! Or a healthy sprinkle of fine dry bread crumbs mixed with grated Parmesan cheese. Or a little lemon juice and grated peel.

- To remove small amounts of liquid fat from food surfaces, blot with paper towels.

- Oversalted soup? Add a teaspoon of sugar and a tablespoon of vinegar to the soup pot, or add a peeled and quartered potato and simmer for 15 minutes.

- To keep eggs from cracking as they boil, pierce the large end with an egg pricker or pin before placing them in boiling water. After boiling eggs, save the water for your spider plants. It contains a mineral that makes them flourish!

❧Microwave Cooking

There are some wonderful advantages to microwave cooking and I've met people all over the country who use this new method and love it. First of all, of course, it is very fast. Most recipes for six people or less cook two to four times faster in microwave than in conventional cooking. My own microwave oven has been a lifesaver many times in my busy schedule. In fact, I rarely cook vegetables and quick-cooking fish any other way.

Microwave also saves energy. The average household uses fifty to eighty-five percent less energy for cooking with microwave. And it helps save human energy, too.

Microwave makes really nutritious foods. Because it cooks so fast and uses little or no water, nutrients are retained, not lost in cooking.

Microwave ovens are almost care-free. Many of them can be set to "tell" the oven to defrost, to begin cooking at medium power, to finish on high power and then to hold the food warm until you're ready for it.

As to utensils, you probably already own a lot of things that can be used in a microwave oven. Metal, glazed glass ceramics, crystal, antique dishes and the like are, of course, *not* suitable. The best material is heat-resistant glass or glass ceramic, though other things, like paper board or plastic wrap or wax paper, can also be used.

Modern cookware will be marked "microwave oven safe" or "For oven and microwave use," or similar language of that sort. To put it more generally, cookware you use in a microwave oven should be heat resistant, nonabsorbent, noninflammable, and it should transmit microwave energy. The rounder the dish the better, and dishes without a center—ring molds, for example—are best for "dense" foods such as cake or meat loaves, which can't be stirred or prearranged.

Browning is, of course, a major concern in using microwave. To get foods brown, either brown quickly on or *in* a regular range, then transfer to the microwave for cooking. OR do the reverse and go from the microwave to a final glazing by conventional means. Browning trays or skillets that are preheated, empty, in the microwave help you get foods to brown without resorting to your regular oven.

Always preheat in the oven, but *never* exceed the time recommended by the manufacturer of your appliance. Butter or margarine will help food brown—and also prevent sticking. Foods at refrigerator temperature will brown better than those that are frozen, and also you will find that drying the food with paper towels before you place it in the oven will help. Then there are all sorts of "slipcovers" to disguise food—everything from sauces to paprika and "paint-on" browners such as Worcestershire or soy sauce.

Stir or rearrange foods while they are cooking to redistribute the heat. Microwave cooks faster along the outer edges of the utensil—the bottom, top and sides—so you'll have to rotate dishes that you don't want to stir—like lasagna, for example. You'll find that large roasts, poultry or big casseroles cook more evenly if you turn them during the cooking process. Shield the thin parts of roasts or poultry and the corners of cakes and breads. Arrange the thick parts toward the outside of your utensil, the thin parts toward the center.

What recipes work in the microwave oven? There are a lot of microwave cookbooks, brochures and magazine articles that will help you, but you can also use the conventional recipes you've been collecting for years—as well as those in this book. All you have to do is to convert those recipes. That process is less complicated than you think. As a general rule, microwave cooking time is one quarter to one third that of conventional cooking for recipes requiring high power, and one third to one half for recipes using medium power.

Cut seasoning quantities in half if they are greater than one teaspoon in the conventional recipe. In fact, I find that it's better to salt foods *after* the cooking is completed.

You can use one third less liquid than in conventional cooking because liquids are not evaporated. Of course, if the food needs to be reconstituted —instant potatoes or rice, for example—you'll need more liquid. By the same token, you really don't have to use fats and oils, which is certainly a big advantage for me.

Use a slightly larger cooking vessel than the conventional recipe calls for, since with such fast cooking food in the microwave may boil over. Prick foods like unpeeled potatoes, egg yolks or sausages or they may burst during cooking.

We've compiled a list of tips that may help you get the most out of this wonderful device. They're tricks that I use all the time:

I. MEATS

- Select a uniformly shaped roast. If one end is smaller, shield it with foil to prevent overcooking. But first, check to see that foil can be used in your oven.
- Meats with even marbling cook more evenly. If the fat cover is heavier in one area, the meat next to it will cook faster and may overcook.
- Boneless meat cooks slower, but more evenly than meats with a bone, since the bone attracts microwave energy.

- To brown large cuts of meat without using a microwave browner, brush with soy sauce, Worcestershire sauce or Micro-Shake® (a browning powder).
- Cured ham, sausage or hot dogs are precooked and need only brief heating. Before heating, prick meats that have a skin.
- Marinate meats as with conventional cooking. In general, decrease the quantity of seasonings when microwaving. Add salt judiciously after cooking, since it tends to draw moisture out of meats.

II. POULTRY

- A whole chicken or smallish turkey is particularly ideal for microwaving since the meat is on the outside and the center is hollow. The maximum size turkey for microwaving is 12 to 14 pounds. Larger birds may not fit in the cavity of your microwave oven.
- Cover thin parts of whole birds such as the tips of legs and wings or the high point of the breast bone with smooth pieces of foil to prevent overcooking. Use foil during first half of cooking time only and only if oven manufacturer recommends its use in your oven.
- Cornish hens and other small birds cook quickly on High (100%) power. Turkeys, ducks and whole chickens do best at Medium (70% to 50%) power.
- For a crispier crust on chicken pieces, coat with crushed fried onion rings, cracker or bread crumbs, corn meal or herb stuffing. Cook on a microwave rack. Rotate dish during cooking.

III. FISH

- Fish cooks quickly and is easy to overcook. When done, it will be flaky and turn opaque in color. Allow 5 to 6 minutes per pound for microwaving fresh or defrosted fish on High power. The center will finish cooking during standing time.
- When using frozen fish, do *not* completely defrost in the microwave oven. Finish defrosting by holding it under cold running water.
- Arrange fish so thicker pieces are toward edge of dish and thinner pieces are toward the center.
- Fish does not reheat well in the microwave oven. It becomes tough and rubbery.
- To remove a fishy odor from the oven cavity, pour ½ cup lemon juice in a liquid measure. Place cup in oven and boil juice on High power for 1½ to 2 minutes. Or, sprinkle a small amount of baking soda on a damp paper towel and wipe the oven cavity.

IV. CASSEROLES

- As a rule of thumb, allow 1½ to 2 minutes of microwaving on High (100%) power per cup of casserole.
- If the mixture cannot be stirred or rearranged, rotate the dish midway through the cooking cycle for even cooking.
- The colder the mixture, the longer the heating time.
- If the edges start to overcook before the center is heated, use a lower power setting or place triangles of foil over the corners of the dish for half of the cooking cycle. Standing time will also help the center finish cooking.
- Prepare the base of a casserole recipe, such as the meat and sauce, ahead of time and freeze. Defrost, add remaining ingredients and heat.

V. EGGS

- In conventional cooking, eggs cook from the white portion to the yolk. In microwave cooking, the opposite is true. An egg yolk contains more fat than the white and therefore attracts more energy and cooks faster.
- Slightly undercook eggs. Let them stand covered for several minutes to complete cooking.
- Never cook an egg in its shell. It will explode.
- Always pierce an egg yolk before poaching or frying.
- If eggs cool before serving, return them to the microwave oven for about 10 to 15 seconds per egg or until hot.

VI. VEGETABLES

- Vegetables are almost always cooked on High (100%) power in a covered container.
- Cream, butter or broth may be substituted for the water.
- Do *not* add salt to vegetables when cooking as it dehydrates and leaches nutrients and moisture from the food.
- For faster, more even cooking, cut vegetables uniformly into small pieces. Stir or rearrange vegetables halfway through cooking cycle.
- Pierce skins of potatoes or squash, allowing steam to vent during cooking. For a tender skin, wrap potato in plastic wrap before cooking. For a crisper skin, wrap in paper towel.
- Broccoli stems can be split to speed their cooking.
- To microwave corn on the cob, place ears in oblong casserole. Cover tightly with plastic wrap and microwave about 1½ to 2 minutes per ear.

VII. SOUPS AND SAUCES

- Microwave clear, brothy soups that contain meats or raw vegetables on High (100%) power.
- Very dense purees, cream soups, seafood chowders or soups containing less tender cuts of meat should all be cooked on Medium (50%) power.
- Cover most soups during heating. Glass covers are ideal.

VIII. LEFTOVERS

- One of the microwave oven's claims to fame is its reheating of leftovers. They often taste as good or better when reheated than when the food was freshly prepared.
- Remember, as quantities increase, heating time increases proportionately or vice versa.
- Slicing, rearranging or stirring helps to reheat leftovers quickly and evenly.
- When reheating several leftovers, start with the one that will require the most microwaving time and finish with the one that is quickest to heat. If the first leftovers have cooled before the remainder are hot, just return them to the microwave oven for a few seconds.
- Refrigerated casseroles require about 1½ to 2 minutes per cup to reheat; meat, 30 seconds to 1 minute per serving; and vegetables, 1 to 1½ minutes per cup.

IX. BREADS AND CAKES

- Since breads and cakes will not brown, enhance their appearance with special toppings—cinnamon-sugar, crushed graham crackers or nuts, frosting, rolled oats, cracker or cookie crumbs or a streusel topping.
- Let cake mix batters stand in the pan for about 10 minutes before cooking to reduce unevenness of the top surface.
- To make a cake or bread easier to unmold, line bottom of dish with wax paper or butter the dish and sprinkle with cinnamon or crumbs prior to filling with cake batter.
- Fill the dish ½ full, not ⅔, since microwaved cakes achieve a greater volume.
- Rotate dish 2 or 3 times during microwaving to prevent overcooked sides or corners. A ring-shaped dish alleviates this problem.
- The top may look moist even when it is done, so check beneath the surface with a toothpick. If the inner cake is done, the top is done.

- Puff pastries and angel food cakes cannot be cooked in the microwave oven. They will rise, but will not develop the crust needed to hold their shape after they are removed from the oven.

X. COOKIES AND PIES

- Microwave cookie dough is stiffer than conventional dough to keep cookies from becoming too thin and tender.
- Cookies and bars cook too fast to develop surface browning. Nuts, spices, sugars and frosting add color.
- If a golden pie crust is preferred, add dark spices, instant coffee grains or cocoa to the crust or use whole-wheat flour.
- Fruit pies have a tendency to boil over. Set pie plate on wax paper in the microwave oven for easy clean up.
- To cook commercially prepared frozen pies, transfer frozen pie to glass pie plate. Microwave on Medium (50%) power until a toothpick can be inserted into center. Finish baking conventionally at suggested temperature for ½ to ⅔ suggested time.

XI. FREEZING

- To avoid tying up your cookware, try one of the following suggestions:
- Freeze food in container. When frozen defrost in microwave oven just enough to unmold. Wrap frozen food in foil or freezer paper, label, and return to freezer.
- Line dish with foil, fill with food, and fold foil over top tightly. Place in freezer. When food is frozen, remove foil-wrapped food, label and return to freezer.
- When reheating frozen foods, stir or rearrange foods if possible to speed and even cooking. When defrosted, place a glass custard cup upright in the middle of the mixture. This allows microwave energy to reach the food from the sides and middle, thus heating the food quicker.
- Add bread or cracker crumbs or cheese toppings to defrosted food just prior to serving. If placed on food before freezing, they may overcook when heated with the other ingredients the entire time.

SOUPS
and STARTERS

GRANDMA'S CHICKEN SOUP

No good cook ever forgets chicken soup. Save vegetable scraps, juices, chicken bones—whatever—and keep them well wrapped in the freezer until it's time to make soup.

Serve chicken soup with cooked rice or fine noodles in it, or use it instead of canned broth as a base for other soups and for sauces. The cooked chicken, an important byproduct of this soup, can be used (or frozen for future use) in a number of dishes—like Chicken Crepes (p. 64) or Chicken Salad Vèronique (p. 137). Or you can put some of it back into the soup before reheating. Do not cover finished chicken soup while it is cooling or it may turn sour.

3- to 5-pound chicken, whole or
   in parts (a stewing chicken is
   best)
1 onion, peeled
2 carrots
2 stalks celery with leaves
Few sprigs fresh dill, tarragon or
   rosemary
Few sprigs fresh parsley
4 whole black peppercorns,
   slightly crushed
Salt

Put all the ingredients into a 5-quart pot, cover with 3 quarts of cold water and simmer until the chicken is cooked through, about 40 minutes. Remove the chicken and let it cool, then remove the chicken meat from the bones. Return the bones and skin to the pot for further gentle simmering, partially covered, about 2 hours in all. Reserve or freeze the cut-up chicken for future use. Strain the soup, discarding the vegetables. Let cool, uncovered; then refrigerate until the fat congeals on the top. Remove the fat before reheating. Chicken soup freezes well and, as Grandma always knew, it's good for everything that ails you.

Six servings.

❧ GREEK LEMON–RICE SOUP

The Greeks call it *avgolemono*—I call it delicious.

5 cups chicken broth
3 tablespoons fresh lemon juice
½ teaspoon dried thyme
¼ cup uncooked white rice (not
   instant)
½ cup plain yogurt
1 clove garlic, minced
1 tablespoon finely chopped fresh
   parsley
Salt
Freshly ground pepper

Combine the chicken broth, lemon juice and thyme in a 4-quart saucepan; bring to a boil. Stir in the rice, cover and simmer over low heat for 20 to 25 minutes or until the rice is tender. While the rice cooks, stir together the yogurt, garlic, parsley and ¼ teaspoon salt. Taste and add more ground pepper until well seasoned. Spoon the soup into bowls, passing the yogurt sauce separately.

Four servings.

❧ GREENHOUSE APPLE SOUP

Chef Helmut Reichart of London's Greenhouse Restaurant gave me this recipe, an unusual dish to spark the appetite. If you can't find red peppers, use 6 green peppers instead.

¼ pound (1 stick) butter
3 green peppers, seeded and
   minced
3 sweet red peppers, seeded and
   minced
3 large yellow onions, sliced thin
1 medium cucumber, peeled,
   seeded and diced
5 green cooking apples, peeled,
   cored and diced
2 ½ cups beef broth
1 cup heavy cream
Salt
Freshly ground pepper
Fried-bread croutons

Melt the butter in a 5-quart saucepan over low heat. Add the peppers, onions, cucumber and apples and sauté until softened, about 10 minutes. Add the broth and cream and simmer for 15 minutes more. Add salt and pepper to taste. Serve in bowls or mugs, sprinkled with croutons.

Eight servings.

❧ CREAM OF TOMATO SOUP

I make this in great quantities during the summer, when days are long and tomatoes plentiful. If you hold off on adding the milk and cream, you can freeze the tomato base for winter feasting. Ripe tomatoes also provide the basis for a great tomato sauce (p. 87). To peel tomatoes, immerse them in boiling water for about 30 seconds, then remove the skins.

1 small onion, sliced thin
1 ½ tablespoons olive oil
1 tablespoon chopped fresh
   parsley
1 teaspoon chopped fresh basil or
   ½ teaspoon dried
1 teaspoon chopped fresh thyme
   or ½ teaspoon dried
Salt
Freshly ground pepper
1 ½ pounds ripe tomatoes, peeled
   and quartered
1 ½ cups chicken broth
½ cup milk
½ cup light cream
Chopped fresh chives

Sauté the onion in the oil, seasoning it with parsley, basil, thyme, salt and pepper. When the onion is soft and translucent but not browned, add the tomatoes and cook for 10 minutes. Add the chicken broth and simmer for 30 minutes or until slightly thickened. Season with salt and pepper, tasting, until the flavors are delicately blended. Puree in a blender or food processor. (You can cool and freeze the soup at this point if you wish.) Add the milk and cream and serve either hot or cold, garnished with chopped chives.

Four servings.

❧ MUSHROOM BISQUE

To present this elegant soup properly, set aside one mushroom cap for each serving. Sauté the mushroom caps in a little butter. When serving, place one in the center of each bowl of soup and sprinkle with some chopped parsley.

1 pound fresh mushrooms
¼ pound (1 stick) butter
1 onion, chopped fine
2 tablespoons sherry or white
  wine
Salt
Freshly ground pepper
6 tablespoons flour
1 quart chicken broth
3 cups milk
1 cup light cream
Chopped fresh parsley

Wash the mushrooms* (or wipe them dry with a damp paper towel if they are not too dirty). Slice or chop, then sauté them in *2 tablespoons* of the butter, together with the onion, until almost dry. Add the sherry and season well with salt and pepper; set aside, but keep it warm. In a 3-quart saucepan, melt the remaining *6 tablespoons* of butter, add the flour and cook over low heat, stirring, for 3 to 4 minutes. Slowly add the chicken broth and cook, stirring, until the sauce reaches the boiling point and thickens. Gradually add the milk and cream, then stir in the mushroom mixture. Serve piping hot, sprinkled with chopped parsley.

Six to eight servings.

Variation:

Substitute 2 cups thinly sliced celery (including some of the tender leaves) for the mushrooms and you'll have Celery Bisque.

---

*I just bought one of those soft-bristled mushroom brushes and, by golly, I use it. Try your local gourmet store, and give your mushrooms the brush-off.

HAM AND OYSTER SOUP

This is a rich, filling soup; make it when you have some leftover ham. You *can* use beef broth, but if there's a leftover ham bone, you can begin by making a ham broth, covering the bone with water and simmering it for a few hours, together with a cut-up onion, a few stalks of celery, a carrot or two and any ham trimmings or pan drippings you may have. If you wish, you can freeze the leftover ham in the ham broth until you're ready to make this soup.

1 small onion, minced
2 tablespoons butter
¼ cup flour
1 cup finely chopped cooked ham
1 quart ham or beef broth
½ cup diced celery
¾ cup uncooked rice
1 bay leaf
1 pint fresh oysters, with liquid
Salt
Freshly ground pepper
2 tablespoons chopped fresh
  parsley

In a 3-quart saucepan, sauté the onion in the butter until tender. Add the flour and cook until delicately browned, stirring all the time over low heat. Add the ham, broth, celery, rice, bay leaf and liquid from the oysters. Cook gently until the rice is done and the celery tender, about 20 minutes. Season with salt and pepper. Add the oysters, either minced or whole, and cook just until the edges curl. Remove the bay leaf, and serve the soup sprinkled with chopped parsley.

Six to eight servings.

❧ DAY-BEFORE LENTIL SOUP

I've dubbed this particular recipe Day-Before Lentil Soup because it should be refrigerated for a day before serving to bring out its robust flavor. Before reheating, I like to puree about one-third of the soup in a blender or food processor to make it thicker. It's a meal in itself; for a meal and a half, add browned kielbasa or any sweet sausage slices or some sliced frankfurters. I've been known to "stretch" this soup by adding 3 to 4 peeled and diced potatoes about 25 to 30 minutes before the soup is done. (You may have to add a bit more water if you try this.)

5 slices bacon, cut into ¼-inch strips
2 medium onions, chopped
1 cup chopped celery (include some leaves)
1 cup chopped carrots
1 can (16 ounces) tomatoes, with liquid
½ teaspoon dried thyme (or more to taste)
½ teaspoon freshly ground pepper
1 bay leaf
1 teaspoon salt (or to taste)
2 cups dried lentils, washed and picked over
2 quarts water
¼ cup wine vinegar
½ cup chopped fresh parsley
2 eggs, hard cooked and chopped fine
Lemon wedges

Cook the bacon in a 5-quart casserole over low heat until nicely browned; remove with a slotted spoon and drain on paper towels. Add the onions to the hot bacon fat and sauté them until they are limp. Add the celery, carrots and tomatoes with liquid, then stir in the seasonings. Add the lentils (there's no need to soak them), the reserved bacon and the water. Bring to a boil, stirring occasionally, then simmer, uncovered, for 30 to 45 minutes, adding a cup or so of water if it seems necessary. When the lentils are just tender, not mushy, remove them from the heat, let cool, cover and refrigerate overnight. Before serving, puree about ⅓ of the soup in a blender or food processor, then heat all the soup slowly over moderate heat, stirring. Remove the bay leaf and stir in the wine vinegar and chopped parsley. Taste and add more seasonings if necessary. Garnish each serving with chopped egg and pass around a plate of lemon wedges.

Eight to ten servings.

❧ VEGETABLE SOUP WITH BASIL

Vegetable soup is delicious and so easy to prepare. Use it at once, or freeze it for the future. Add tiny meat balls in addition to the beef for a nice variation, cooking them in the soup for about 20 minutes before serving.

¼ pound lean ground beef
2 medium onions, diced
1 clove garlic, minced
1 tablespoon oil
1 quart water
Salt
Freshly ground pepper
1 ½ teaspoons chopped fresh basil
*   or ½ teaspoon dried*
½ cup chopped celery (include
*   some leaves)*
½ cup canned tomatoes, drained
4 large carrots, sliced
1 pound small new potatoes,
*   peeled and quartered*
About ¼ teaspoon hot pepper
*   sauce*

Sauté the meat, onion and garlic in oil over moderate heat in a 2-quart saucepan for about 5 minutes. Add the water and the remaining ingredients, cover and bring to a boil over high heat. Reduce the heat and simmer for 30 minutes or until the carrots and potatoes are tender. Add hot pepper sauce to taste.

Six servings.

❧ MANHATTAN CLAM CHOWDER

Why do I enjoy this when any New Englander will tell you it's white clam chowder or nothing? I was born in Manhattan, what can I tell you?

4 slices bacon, cut into ¼-inch strips
1 clove garlic, minced
½ cup finely chopped onion
½ cup chopped green pepper
½ cup diced carrots
¼ cup chopped celery
3 cups peeled, diced potatoes
Salt
6 cups boiling water
2 quarts fresh clams, shucked, with liquid, or *4 cans (7½ ounces each) minced clams, with liquid*
1 cup chopped tomatoes (canned or fresh)
¼ cup tomato paste
1½ teaspoons dried thyme
Freshly ground pepper
1 bay leaf
4 whole cloves

In a 5-quart Dutch oven over moderate heat, cook the bacon until crisp, about 6 to 8 minutes. Add the garlic and onion and cook until the onion is golden. Add the green pepper, carrots, celery, potatoes, salt and water, cover and bring to a boil. Reduce the heat and simmer for 20 minutes. Add the remaining ingredients and continue simmering for 10–15 minutes more. Remove the bay leaf and serve.

Twelve servings.

❦ QUICK SPINACH SOUP

This soup is good either hot or cold. It's also good for the waistline if you leave out the cream. I like it before a light entrée, especially chicken or fish.

¾ pound fresh spinach
¼ cup chopped green onion
1 quart chicken broth
4 tablespoons (½ stick) butter
2 tablespoons flour
1 to 2 teaspoons fresh lemon juice
Salt
Freshly ground pepper
1 cup light cream (optional)
Nutmeg

Simmer the spinach and onion in the broth for about 10 minutes or until the onion is soft. Puree in a blender or food processor. Melt the butter in a 2½-quart saucepan, stir in the flour and cook over low heat, stirring constantly, for 3 to 4 minutes. Gradually stir in the spinach puree and cook, stirring, until the soup reaches the boiling point and thickens. Add the lemon juice and salt and pepper to taste. Stir in the cream if desired, and garnish with a light dusting of nutmeg.

Six servings.

❦ GAZPACHO WITH YOGURT

This is my idea of a perfect summer soup. It's not only cool and refreshing, but there's no cooking required, no standing over a hot stove. To peel tomatoes, place them in boiling water for a few seconds, then remove the skins with a sharp knife.

4 to 5 ripe tomatoes,* peeled
1 large cucumber, peeled and
  seeded
1 large onion, quartered
1 green pepper, seeded and
  halved
2 cloves garlic, chopped
3 cups tomato juice
⅓ cup olive oil
⅓ cup red wine vinegar
¼ teaspoon hot pepper sauce
½ cup plain yogurt
Salt
Freshly ground pepper

In a blender† or food processor, combine 2 of the tomatoes, ½ of the cucumber, ½ of the onion, ½ of the green pepper, the garlic, and 1 cup of the tomato juice. Blend until the vegetables are pureed. In a large serving bowl, mix the pureed vegetables with the remaining tomato juice, the olive oil, vinegar, hot pepper sauce, yogurt, salt and pepper. Cover and refrigerate until chilled, about 2 hours. Chop the remaining tomatoes, cucumber, onion and green pepper and add them to the soup before serving.

Six servings.

---

*If luscious, fresh tomatoes aren't available, use the equivalent in drained, imported canned tomatoes.
†If you intend to use a blender, you will have to precut the vegetables fairly small.

❦ COLD CARROT SOUP

Here's a rich, golden soup that I call 14-carrot cold. As healthy as it is delicious, it's also good hot, served with a dollop of sour cream.

3 tablespoons butter
1 stalk celery with leaves,
*   chopped fine*
1 ½ cups finely chopped onion
1 ½ pounds carrots, cut into ¼-
*   inch rounds*
2 medium potatoes, peeled and
*   diced*
1 teaspoon sugar
1 tablespoon chopped fresh dill
*   or 1 teaspoon dried*
3 cups chicken broth
1 cup milk
1 cup cream
Pinch of cayenne
Salt
Freshly ground pepper
Chopped fresh parsley

Melt the butter in a 3-quart saucepan. Add the celery and onion and cook over low heat until the onion is translucent. Add the carrots, potatoes, sugar, dill and broth. Cook, covered, over low heat for 25 minutes or until the vegetables are very tender. Let cool slightly, then puree in a blender or food processor. Cover and chill (or freeze for later use). Just before serving add the milk, cream, cayenne, salt and pepper. Check the seasonings. Garnish with parsley.

Eight servings.

❧ CUCUMBER VICHYSSOISE

This soup is the perfect beginning for a midsummer night's barbecue. It can also be the centerpiece for a high-noon lunch, spooned from a large glass bowl and surrounded by assorted sandwich quarters. Or use it to fill the family thermos for a very special picnic.

2 medium potatoes, peeled and
* cut into ½-inch cubes*
1 small onion, chopped
2 or 3 cucumbers, peeled, seeded
* and sliced (about 1 ½ cups)*
1 teaspoon dried dill
3 cups chicken broth
½ cup plain yogurt
2 tablespoons fresh lemon juice
Salt
Freshly ground pepper
Thin cucumber slices*
Chopped green onion

Place the potatoes, onion, cucumbers, dill and chicken broth in a 3-quart saucepan and bring to a boil. Reduce the heat and cook for about 15 minutes or until the vegetables are just done. Let cool. Puree in a blender or food processor. Fold in the yogurt and lemon juice, and add salt and pepper to taste. Chill for at least 4 hours. Serve the soup in chilled cups garnished with cucumber slices and chopped green onion.

Four to six servings.

---

*If the cucumbers are unwaxed, leave the skins on and score lengthwise with a fork or knife before slicing into rounds.

❧ SHRIMP-STUFFED TOMATOES

Easy to prepare in advance, Shrimp-Stuffed Tomatoes are a lovely luncheon dish. They also add color and contrast to a buffet table. Freeze the tomato pulp for use in Homemade Tomato Sauce (p. 87) or Cream of Tomato Soup (p. 21).

4 small ripe tomatoes
1 ½ cups chopped, cooked fresh
  shrimp or 2 cans (4 ¼
  ounces) tiny shrimp, drained
2 green onions, chopped fine
2 tablespoons butter, softened
Handful of chopped fresh parsley
1 small clove garlic, minced
2 ounces cream cheese, softened
Dollop of Dijon-style mustard
1 teaspoon fresh lemon juice
Salt
Freshly ground pepper

Slice off the tops of the tomatoes and scoop out the pulp; invert over paper towels to drain for 10 minutes or more. Combine the remaining ingredients, tasting and adding more seasonings until you like the flavor. Use the mixture to stuff the tomatoes. Serve cold.

Four servings.

Variations:

Substitute chopped cooked ham, bacon, turkey or chicken for the shrimp.

❧ POTTED CHEESE

I like to serve this tangy cheese spread with crackers and raw vegetables before dinner. It will keep for days in the refrigerator, but bring it to room temperature before serving for easy spreading. It makes a great gift packed into pretty glass dishes and garnished with lots of chopped fresh parsley. (Include the recipe when you give the cheese.)

8 ounces sharp Cheddar cheese
4 ounces cream cheese
1 ½ tablespoons finely chopped
   green onions
1 ½ teaspoons chopped fresh
   parsley
½ teaspoon dry mustard
¼ cup beer
½ teaspoon celery seed
Dash of hot pepper sauce
1 to 2 cloves garlic, minced
Salt (optional)

Grate the Cheddar cheese while it is still cold, then let both cheeses come to room temperature. Using an electric beater or a wooden spoon, combine the cheeses with the remaining ingredients, mixing until light and fluffy. Taste for salt and add it if it seems necessary. Pack into a serving container and chill.

Twelve ounces.

Variations:

Use robust red wine instead of beer, or substitute poppy or dill seed for celery seed.

❧ GUACAMOLE SALAD

Garnish this with pimiento, olives, parsley, tomato wedges or chunks of fresh avocado (dipped in lemon juice) for a colorful work of art.

1 clove garlic, halved
1 ripe avocado
1 to 2 tablespoons fresh lime or
   lemon juice
2 teaspoons finely grated onion
Salt
Dash of hot pepper sauce
1 ripe tomato, peeled and
   chopped
Lettuce leaves
Corn chips

Rub the inside of a serving bowl with the garlic; discard the garlic. Peel the avocado and mash it in the bowl with a fork. Stir in the lime or lemon juice, onion, salt and hot pepper sauce. Mix, adding enough pepper sauce to make it really lively. Just before serving, fold in the tomato. To serve, place the bowl on a platter surrounded by crisp lettuce leaves, topped with corn chips for dipping.

Four to six servings.

o❧o CURRIED CAPONATA

This spread will keep for days in the refrigerator. Bring it to room temperature before serving on crackers or party rye bread. I know the curry flavor isn't traditional, but it adds zip.

¼ cup olive oil
1 medium eggplant, peeled and
    diced
1 teaspoon curry powder
1 cup chopped onion
½ cup minced celery
1 cup canned or fresh tomato
    puree
⅓ cup chopped pitted green olives
2 tablespoons drained capers
2 tablespoons red wine or cider
    vinegar
1 tablespoon sugar
Salt
Freshly ground pepper
2 tablespoons chopped fresh
    parsley

Heat *3 tablespoons* of the oil in 2-quart saucepan. Add the eggplant and the curry powder. Cook over moderate heat, stirring occasionally, until the eggplant pieces are almost translucent. Add the remaining *1 tablespoon* of oil and the onion and celery. Cook, stirring, until the onion is limp. Add the tomato puree, olives, capers, vinegar and sugar. Sprinkle lightly with salt and pepper; stir gently to combine. Cover and simmer, stirring occasionally, for 30 minutes to 1 hour, until very thick; add water only if necessary. Taste and add more seasonings if necessary. Stir in the parsley. Let cool, then refrigerate until needed.

About three cups.

Variations:

Use Curried Caponata as a filling for omelets or crepes (p. 64). Or dust with freshly grated Parmesan cheese, and you'll have a great luncheon dish.

❦ BACON-AND-WATER-CHESTNUT TIDBITS

No point in giving quantities here. Make as many as you think you will need, but be forewarned: These are so good, there will never be enough!

Canned water chestnuts
Brown sugar
Bacon slices
Soy sauce

Preheat the oven to 425° F. Drain the water chestnuts, rinse them in cold water and pat dry. Roll each water chestnut in brown sugar. Cut the bacon slices in half, wrap each half around a water chestnut and secure it with a toothpick. Sprinkle with soy sauce. Place in a shallow baking dish and bake in the oven, turning occasionally, until the bacon is crisp, about 20 to 30 minutes. Drain on paper towels and serve at once.

❦ CREAMED DEVILED EGGS

6 eggs, hard cooked
3 tablespoons mayonnaise
Salt
Freshly ground pepper
3 tablespoons butter
3 tablespoons flour
½ teaspoon prepared mustard
⅛ teaspoon dried marjoram
1 cup milk
1 cup shredded Swiss cheese
Pimiento strips (optional)

Preheat the oven to 350° F. Peel and halve the eggs, then remove the yolks. Place the yolks in a small mixing bowl. Add the mayonnaise and salt and pepper, tasting and mixing well. Stuff the eggs with the yolk mixture and arrange in a baking dish. Melt the butter in a small saucepan over low heat. Stir in the flour, season with salt, mustard and marjoram and cook over low heat, stirring constantly for 3 to 4 minutes. Stir in the milk, and cook, stirring constantly, until the mixture reaches the boiling point and thickens. Spoon this sauce around the eggs and sprinkle the cheese over all. Bake for about 10 minutes or until the sauce is bubbly. Garnish with pimiento strips, if desired. Serve immediately.

Four servings.

❧ BILL DOLLARD'S SCOTCH EGGLETS

5 small eggs, hard cooked
2 (12 ounces each) packages hot
  or mild bulk pork sausage or
  ¾ pound Italian sweet
  sausage, casing removed, or a
  combination of sweet and hot
2 large eggs, lightly beaten
1 cup bread crumbs with Italian
  seasonings*
Vegetable or corn oil

**MUSTARD–MAYONNAISE
SAUCE:**

2 cups mayonnaise
2 tablespoons finely chopped
  drained capers
2 tablespoons chopped fresh
  parsley
1 tablespoon fresh lemon juice
2 tablespoons Dijon-style
  mustard

Slice off the rounded ends of the hard-cooked eggs. You can chop and use them in salad later. Then peel and slice each hard-cooked egg into 3 or 4 thick slices. Enclose a slice of egg in a thin coating of sausage meat, being sure that the top and sides of the egg slice are covered. Repeat this process for each egg slice. Dip each patty into beaten egg, then dip it into bread crumbs, coating the patty evenly. Refrigerate for 30 minutes to help the crumbs adhere. In a 10-inch skillet over medium-low heat, fry the patties in oil until browned and well done. You can either eat them as you make them or else refrigerate them first, but do remove them from the refrigerator 30 minutes before serving so that the eggs can return to room temperature. Make Mustard–Mayonnaise Sauce by thoroughly beating all the ingredients together; serve this sauce with the egglets.

Fifteen to twenty patties.

---

*If you cannot find this product in the store, simply add a little oregano and basil to unseasoned crumbs.

❦ MARINATED MUSHROOMS

I use just the mushroom caps in this dish because they look so pretty. But I save the stems to use in Brown Rice with Mushrooms (p. 82) or Mushroom Bisque (p. 22).

1 pound fresh mushrooms
⅔ cup white or cider vinegar
½ cup olive oil
1 clove garlic, minced
1 tablespoon sugar
2 tablespoons sherry
Dash of freshly ground pepper
Dash of hot pepper sauce
1 sweet onion, sliced into thin
  rings
Watercress or leaf lettuce

Wash and dry the mushrooms or wipe them clean with a damp paper towel. Remove the stems, setting them aside for use in another dish. Combine all the ingredients except the mushrooms, onion slices and watercress; mix thoroughly. Add the mushrooms and onions and stir. Refrigerate for at least 5 hours, stirring occasionally. Serve on a bed of watercress or lettuce or serve plain, on toothpicks.

Four to six servings.

❦ CHICKEN–WALNUT PÂTÉ

½ cup walnuts
1 cup diced cooked chicken or
  turkey
3 ounces cream cheese, cut into
  chunks and softened
½ clove garlic, minced
3 tablespoons mayonnaise
2 teaspoons fresh dill or 1
  teaspoon dried
Salt
Watercress or lettuce
3 sprigs fresh parsley, chopped
  fine
Crackers or rounds of French
  bread

Chop the walnuts in a blender or food processor, turning the motor on and off until the nuts are chopped fine. Add the chicken, cream cheese and garlic to the blender or processor; blend just until smooth. Add the mayonnaise, dill and salt and blend again. Form into a ball and arrange on watercress or lettuce leaves. Sprinkle with chopped parsley. Serve with crackers or bread.

Variations:

Use pecans instead of walnuts, or substitute tarragon for the dill.

❧ Other Starter Suggestions

In addition to the recipes in this chapter, there are a number of other recipes in this book that provide excellent beginnings for a meal. You may have to reduce the quantities in some cases, for you will certainly want to serve small portions. That should be true of any appetizer you serve—it's meant to whet the appetite, not to satisfy it.

Here are a few appetizer suggestions from recipes that appear in other chapters of this book:

Ham Balls in Orange Sauce (p. 52)
Chicken Teriyaki Skewers (p. 63)
Chicken Crepes (p. 64)
Fish Vinaigrette (p. 75)
Sherried Shrimp (p. 77)
Shellfish Ramekins (p. 78)
Pasta and Clams (p. 89)
Poached Eggs in Tomato Sauce (p. 97)
Tomato–Onion Quiche (p. 105)
Zucchini–Mushroom Quiche (p. 106)
Cheese Soufflé (p. 109)
Green Beans Vinaigrette (p. 114)
Fried Mushrooms (p. 119)
Spinach Crepes (p. 125)
Broiled Tomatoes with Fresh Herbs (p. 128)
Breaded Zucchini Circles (p. 129)
Italian Tomato Salad (p. 134)
Cheese Wafers (p. 143)

MEAT

❧ HERBED ROAST BEEF WITH OVEN-BROWNED POTATOES

The larger the roast, the more good leftovers you'll have. Use them in Leftover Beef with Mushroom Sauce (see below), Beef Salad Parisienne (p. 135), or see Using Leftovers (p. 180).

One 3- to 5-pound eye round
  roast
1 clove garlic, minced
1 tablespoon finely chopped fresh
  parsley
1 tablespoon finely chopped fresh
  chives or green onion
1 teaspoon of a mixture of
  thyme, marjoram and
  rosemary
1 teaspoon salt
1 tablespoon Dijon-style mustard
18 small whole new potatoes,
  peeled and cooked
White wine (optional)

Preheat the oven to 325° F. Place the meat in a roasting pan. Mix the remaining ingredients (except the potatoes and white wine) into a paste and spread over the beef. Roast for 20 to 25 minutes per pound or until the internal temperature on a meat thermometer registers 140° F for rare, 160° F for medium or 170° F for well done. About 30 minutes before the beef is finished, add the potatoes, turning them in the drippings to coat them on all sides and cooking until golden brown. If there aren't enough drippings in the pan to coat the potatoes, add a little water or white wine.

Six servings.

❧ LEFTOVER BEEF WITH MUSHROOM SAUCE

Serve this with rice or noodles or with Barley Casserole (p. 85). For a complete meal, why not add a package of frozen pea pods to the pan during the last 5 minutes of cooking?

½ pound fresh mushrooms, sliced
  thick
2 teaspoons butter
About 2 pounds leftover boiled
  beef (p. 40)
1 tablespoon arrowroot or
  cornstarch
¾ cup beef broth or reduced
  stock from Boiled Beef with
  Vegetables (p. 40)
¼ cup red wine

In a shallow 2½-quart saucepan, sauté the mushrooms in the butter. Dice the beef and add it to the pan. Stir the arrowroot or cornstarch into the broth or stock, then add it and the wine to the pan. Stir until thickened, then simmer, covered, for 5 to 10 minutes.

Four servings.

❧ BOILED BEEF WITH VEGETABLES

I like to make this dish in two steps, often a day or two apart, since it's easy to slice the meat and to degrease the stock after they have been refrigerated for a while. Plan to make more than you need for one meal: The stock and meat can be used in soups, sandwiches and a variety of dishes all week long.

STEP 1

One 3 ½-pound boneless round,
* rump or chuck roast*
1 pound beef or veal neckbones
3 medium onions, 1 studded
* with 3 whole cloves*
3 large carrots, cut into chunks
4 large cloves garlic, unpeeled
1 bay leaf
1 apple, halved
8 to 10 black peppercorns,
* slightly crushed*
About 6 cups cold water

Place the meat and all the other ingredients into a 5-quart casserole and cover with at least 6 cups water. Bring to a boil, skimming off the scum that will rise to the surface, then simmer for 2 to 3 hours or until the meat is very tender. Remove from the heat and strain, discarding all but the meat and stock. Let cool, then refrigerate the meat. Refrigerate the stock: When the fat has risen to the top, degrease. (The meat and stock can be frozen at this point for use in the future.)

STEP 2

4 carrots, cut into chunks
12 small white onions, peeled*
12 small potatoes, peeled
4 medium white turnips, peeled,
* quartered and cored*
1 small cabbage, cored and
* quartered*
Horseradish (freshly grated if
* possible) or Horseradish Sauce*
* (p. 77)*

Cover the carrots, onions, potatoes and turnips with about 2 cups of the stock and cook at a slow boil for about 25 minutes or until done. Boil the cabbage separately in a little stock for about 10 minutes; it should still be crisp. Slice enough beef for 4 servings, place it in a heatproof serving dish, cover with a little hot stock, and surround it with the cooked vegetables. Cover, reheat in a 300° F oven and serve, accompanied by horseradish.

Four to six servings.

---

*To peel white onions, cover them with boiling water for 2 minutes, drain, then peel.

❧ REUBEN CASSEROLE

Serve this with Rye Biscuits (p. 144).

*About 2 pounds fresh or canned
  sauerkraut*
4 slices bacon, chopped
3 tablespoons apple juice
1 onion, chopped
1 apple, peeled and diced
½ teaspoon caraway seed
2 medium ripe tomatoes, sliced
2 tablespoons Russian dressing
*8 large slices cold cooked corned
  beef*
*2 cups shredded Swiss or
  Cheddar cheese*

Preheat the oven to 400° F. Wash the sauerkraut, drain it and squeeze it dry. In a 10-inch skillet, sauté the bacon until crisp. Add the sauerkraut and continue to sauté until the sauerkraut is lightly browned. Add the apple juice, onion, apple and caraway seed. Cover and allow to steam briefly over low heat while you assemble the rest of the ingredients. Spread the sauerkraut mixture over the bottom of an 8-by12-inch baking dish. Top with the tomato slices. Spread the Russian dressing on top of the tomatoes. Cover with the corned beef slices, sprinkle with cheese and bake for about 10 minutes or until heated through.

Four to six servings.

◦✿◦ BEEF CURRY

Serve this over rice with a festive selection of condiments, such as chopped dried apricots, chopped peanuts or slivered almonds, sliced bananas, flaked coconut, raisins and, of course, mango chutney. You can substitute chicken or pork for the beef in this recipe.

2 pounds top sirloin or round steak, cut into 1-inch cubes
⅓ cup flour
3 tablespoons oil
2 large onions, sliced thick
1 clove garlic, minced
¼ teaspoon freshly ground pepper
½ teaspoon powdered ginger
1 teaspoon crushed hot red pepper flakes (or to taste)
1 tablespoon curry powder (or to taste)
1 can (28 ounces) whole tomatoes, with liquid
½ pound sliced fresh mushrooms, sautéed in a little butter

Toss the meat in the flour, shaking off the excess. In a 3-quart saucepan, sauté the meat in the oil until browned. Add the onions, garlic, seasonings and tomatoes with liquid, breaking up the tomatoes as you add them. Cover and cook over low heat until tender, about 2 hours for beef or pork, less for chicken. Add the sautéed mushrooms, stir and serve.

Four to six servings.

❧ CORNELIUS'S CHILI

Here's my favorite chili recipe, made with beef and corn and lots of peppy seasonings. Serve it in deep dishes with rice and a good bitey slaw.

¼ cup vegetable or corn oil
3 medium onions, chopped
3 cloves garlic, minced
3 pounds beef for stewing, cut into ½-inch cubes
3 tablespoons chili powder
¼ cup flour
1 green pepper, minced
2 teaspoons chopped canned jalapeño peppers
1 teaspoon cumin seed
1 teaspoon dried oregano
1 teaspoon celery seed
1 bay leaf
1 can (28 ounces) Italian plum tomatoes, with liquid
1 can (10 ounces) beef broth
2 cups fresh corn kernels or 2 packages (10 ounces each) frozen corn, thawed
1 cup sliced pitted black olives
Salt
Freshly ground pepper

Preheat the oven to 250° F. Heat the oil in a large skillet and lightly sauté the onions and garlic, then remove to a 5-quart saucepan. In the same skillet, lightly brown the meat and add it to the saucepan. Mix the chili powder and flour and blend this into the meat-onion mixture. Add all the other ingredients except the corn, olives, salt and pepper. Bring to a boil, stirring constantly. Transfer to the oven and bake, covered, for 2 to 3 hours or until the meat is tender. Add the remaining ingredients and bake, covered, for 10 minutes more.

Six to eight servings.

✺ PIQUANT PICADILLO

This is a quick, cheap, easy-to-prepare dish with a South-of-the-border flavor. I serve it over rice or on warm tortillas or as a filling for tacos. A salad of leafy greens with sesame seeds and Basic Vinaigrette Dressing (p. 133) is good with it.

2 tablespoons vegetable or corn oil
2 large cloves garlic, minced
1 large onion, chopped coarse
Salt
Freshly ground pepper
1 pound lean ground beef
⅓ cup white wine
2 large ripe tomatoes, peeled and chopped, or 4 canned tomatoes, drained
½ cup raisins, plumped in hot water
⅓ cup sliced pimiento-stuffed olives
1 large green pepper, seeded and cut into strips

Heat the oil in a 10-inch skillet, add the garlic and onion and cook, stirring, for 5 minutes. Add the salt, pepper, meat and wine and cook, stirring, just until the meat is cooked through. Add the tomatoes, raisins and olives and heat. Add the green pepper a few minutes before serving; it should be hot but still green and crisp.

Four to six servings.

BEEF PATTIES WITH SHERRY–CREAM SAUCE

BEEF MIXTURE:

2 pounds ground beef
1 egg
½ cup seasoned bread crumbs
2 tablespoons chopped onion
Salt
Freshly ground pepper
1 tablespoon Worcestershire sauce
1 clove garlic, minced
1 teaspoon dried rosemary,
*   crumbled*
2–3 tablespoons butter

SAUCE:

½ cup sour cream
¼ cup sherry
1 tablespoon fresh lemon juice
1 tablespoon brandy or cognac
Freshly ground pepper
Chopped fresh parsley

Lightly mix all the ingredients but the butter and form the mixture into 8 patties, each 1 ½ inches thick. Heat the butter in a large skillet, and sear the patties on both sides, then reduce the heat and cook to the desired degree of doneness. Remove the patties to a warm serving platter and keep warm. Over low heat, scrape and loosen the pan drippings, using a wooden spoon or spatula. Add the sour cream, sherry, lemon juice and brandy or cognac, seasoning with pepper to taste. Cook for about 3 minutes, then pour this sauce over the patties and serve, garnished with chopped parsley.

Four servings.

❦ BEEF, PORK AND SPINACH TERRINE

This lovely meat loaf, served cold with tiny pickles or cherry peppers, is a perfect buffet or luncheon dish. Makes a good sandwich, too, with a dollop of chili sauce.

2 packages (10 ounces each) frozen chopped spinach
1 ½ pounds lean ground beef
¾ pound lean ground pork
2 cloves garlic, chopped fine
1 medium onion, chopped fine
1 teaspoon freshly ground pepper
1 bay leaf, crumbled
½ teaspoon dried crumbled thyme
½ cup dry bread crumbs
2 eggs
2 slices bacon

Preheat the oven to 325° F. Thaw the spinach and squeeze it dry. Mix all the ingredients, except the bacon, lightly and thoroughly. Fill a loaf pan with the mixture and arrange the bacon slices on top. Bake for 1½ to 1¾ hours or until cooked through. Remove from the oven and pour off the excess fat. Serve warm in thin slices, or cover with foil and weight with heavy cans until ready to serve cold.

Six main-course servings.

❦ MARINATED PORK ROAST

Start this the night before or early in the day.

One 5- to 6-pound center-cut loin of pork, boned

MARINADE:

½ cup soy sauce
½ cup bourbon
2 cloves garlic, minced
3 tablespoons brown sugar
3 tablespoons dry mustard
1–2 tablespoons finely diced fresh ginger or 1 teaspoon powdered

Trim the pork roast of all but ¼ inch of fat; no need to remove the skin. Mix the marinade ingredients together. Put the meat with the marinade into a tight-fitting plastic bag and seal; this way the marinade will cover all sides of the meat, and you won't have to keep turning it. Marinate overnight or for at least 6 hours.

Preheat the oven to 350° F. Drain the roast, reserving the marinade. Bake for 1¼ hours, basting 4 or 5 times with the marinade. Let rest for about 10 minutes before carving into thin slices. Heat the remaining marinade and serve as gravy.

Eight servings.

❧ PARTY PORK ROAST WITH MUSHROOM STUFFING

Serve this with whole cranberry relish, orange slices and buttered white turnips. In this dish, the stuffing is added after the roast is almost finished.

One 3- to 3 ½-pound boneless pork loin roast, well trimmed

STUFFING:

6 ounces firm white bread
5 ounces fresh mushrooms
2 tablespoons chopped green onions
3 to 4 sprigs fresh parsley
½ teaspoon dried thyme
¾ teaspoon dried sage
2 teaspoons grated orange peel
4 thin slices ham
1 tablespoon red wine or sherry

Preheat the oven to 400° F. Put the roast into a roasting pan, place it in the oven and immediately reduce the heat to 325° F. Cook, uncovered, for 30 to 35 minutes per pound or until a meat thermometer registers 170° F. The meat should be cooked through but moist.

While the meat is cooking, make the stuffing, using a food processor or blender. (If you're using a blender, you'll have to cut up the ingredients fairly small.) Process the bread until you have fine crumbs; pour into a bowl and set aside. Add to the blender or processor all the remaining ingredients except the wine or sherry. Process lightly, turning on and off, just until chopped. Mix this into the bread crumbs, then add the wine or sherry.

When the roast is done, remove it from the oven and let stand for 10 to 20 minutes. Cut the meat into ½-inch slices. Starting with the end piece, cover the surface of the slice with stuffing, place it on edge in an 8-inch-square pan or a loaf pan; add the next slice and coat it with stuffing. Reshape the roast, coating each slice of meat with stuffing and placing one slice of meat against the next. Coat the surface of the roast with any remaining stuffing. Return it all to the oven for 10 to 15 minutes, long enough for the flavors to blend together, then remove and serve.

Six servings.

◦🌿◦ PORK CHOPS WITH HARD CIDER

Here's an easy pork dinner that can be baking away in the oven when your guests arrive. Serve with Steamed Cabbage (p. 116).

3 tablespoons vegetable or corn oil
4 1-inch-thick pork chops (about 3 pounds), trimmed
1 large clove garlic, halved
2 large onions, chopped coarse
1 cup uncooked rice
2 medium apples, peeled and sliced
2 ½ cups chicken broth
½ cup hard cider or *regular cider plus 1 tablespoon cider vinegar*
¼ teaspoon powdered cloves
1 small bay leaf
Salt
Freshly ground pepper

Preheat the oven to 350° F. Heat the oil in a shallow casserole. Rub the chops with the cut side of the garlic, then brown them in the oil; remove the chops from the casserole. In the remaining oil, sauté the onions until limp but not brown. Add the chops and top with the onions. Spoon the rice over the chops, then top with the apple slices. In a 1-quart saucepan, bring the broth, cider and seasonings to a boil, then pour the mixture over the chops. Cover and bake for about 45 minutes.

Four servings.

BAVARIAN PORK

I like to serve this with flat noodles or German *spaetzle.*

2 tablespoons vegetable or corn oil
1 pound boneless lean pork
Salt
½ teaspoon freshly ground
    pepper
3 medium potatoes, peeled and
    cut into 1-inch cubes
4 carrots, cut into ¼-inch
    diagonal slices
1 can (10¼ ounces) chicken
    broth
½ cup white wine or water
1 bay leaf
1 teaspoon crumbled dried thyme
2 medium onions, halved and
    sliced thin
½ teaspoon caraway seed
1 tablespoon flour
½ cup sour cream
½ cup chopped fresh parsley

Heat the oil in a 10-inch skillet over moderate heat. Slice the pork thin across the grain and cut it into 2-by-1-inch strips. Season with salt and pepper and brown a few pieces at a time; set aside. While the pork strips are browning, combine the potatoes, carrots, chicken broth, wine or water, bay leaf and thyme in a 2½-quart saucepan and simmer, covered, for 10 minutes. When the pork is browned, remove it from the skillet, scraping any bits free from the bottom of the skillet with a wooden spoon or spatula. Add the onions and caraway seeds to the skillet. Stir gently, cover and cook over moderate heat for 10 minutes, then return the pork to the skillet. Sprinkle with the flour and stir to blend. With a slotted spoon remove the vegetables from the saucepan and add to the skillet along with ½ cup of the cooking broth. Stir, cover and cook for 5 minutes more until pork is cooked through. Mix another ½ cup of the cooking broth with the sour cream and parsley and stir into the meat and vegetable mixture. Simmer, uncovered, for 5 minutes.

Four servings.

❧ SECOND-DAY SPARERIBS

I call these "second-day," because they're best when they've had a chance to marinate overnight. Serve with Corn Pancakes (p. 118) and applesauce.

*1 to 2 tablespoons vegetable or
  corn oil*
*2 ½ to 3 pounds spareribs, cut
  into serving pieces*
½ cup sliced onions
½ cup catsup
¼ cup plain or cider vinegar
2 tablespoons brown sugar
1 tablespoon Worcestershire sauce
1 teaspoon dry mustard
½ teaspoon paprika
½ cup water

Heat the oil in a 10-inch oven-proof skillet over moderate heat; add the spareribs and brown on all sides. Add the sliced onions and cook for 2 minutes, stirring; remove from the heat. Combine the remaining ingredients and pour over the spareribs. Marinate in the refrigerator, covered, for at least 2 hours or overnight.

Preheat the oven to 350° F. Place the covered skillet in the oven and bake for 1¾ hours, spooning the sauce over the spareribs 2 or 3 times during baking. Uncover and crisp them under the broiler for 5 minutes before serving. Watch to see that they don't burn.

Five or six servings.

❧ BROILED HAM SLICES WITH FRESH PEACHES OR PEARS

If you have any ham left over, save it to make Ham Balls in Orange Sauce (p. 52) or Ham and Oyster Soup (p. 23).

1 slice ham (¾ to 1 inch thick)
*2 large fresh peaches or pears,
  halved and pitted*
¼ teaspoon powdered cinnamon
*1 can (1 pound) dark sweet
  pitted cherries, well drained*

Place the ham on a broiler-safe platter. Set it on the broiler rack about 3 inches from the source of heat and broil for 9 to 10 minutes or until the ham is slightly browned. Remove the platter from the broiler. Turn the ham slice over and arrange the peach or pear halves, cut side *up,* at each end of the platter. Sprinkle the cinnamon over the fruit, then spoon the cherries into the cavities. Return the platter to the broiler and continue broiling for about 10 minutes or until the ham is browned on the other side.

Four servings.

CORNELIUS'S CHOUCROUTE GARNIE

An informal party dish with a long life.

¼ *pound bacon, cut into 1-inch*
    pieces
1 pound Polish kielbasa sausage,
    cut into 2-inch pieces
8 pork chops, trimmed and boned
1 ½ cups chopped onions
2 cloves garlic, minced
4 pounds sauerkraut, rinsed and
    drained well
2 medium apples, peeled and
    chopped
1 cup apple cider or juice
½ cup white wine
1 bay leaf
1 ½ teaspoons caraway seed
Freshly ground pepper
4 large potatoes, peeled and diced
8 slices French bread, spread
    with butter and mustard

Preheat the oven to 375° F. Sauté the bacon in a 5-quart saucepan; remove with a slotted spoon and reserve. Brown the meats separately in the bacon fat; remove and reserve. Add the onions and garlic and cook until wilted. Add the cooked bacon, the sauerkraut, apples, cider or juice, wine and seasonings. Bury the cooked meats and the potatoes in the mixture. Cover and place in the oven for 1 ¾ to 2 hours. Place the bread, buttered side *up,* on top of the sauerkraut. Return, uncovered, to the oven for 15 minutes more or until the top is golden.

Eight servings.

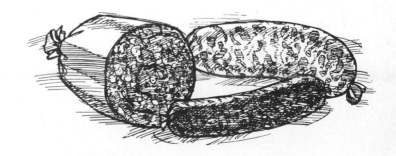

HAM BALLS IN ORANGE SAUCE

This is a favorite dish I've used in numerous cooking demonstrations. Great for buffets, these ham balls are also a sensation at brunches, served with icy melon wedges, eggs and biscuits. Just make them smaller and they make a wonderful predinner hors d'oeuvre.

1 pound ground ham
½ pound ground pork
½ cup cracker crumbs
½ cup finely chopped onion
½ teaspoon dry mustard
½ cup milk
2 eggs
⅓ cup firmly packed brown sugar
1 ½ tablespoons cornstarch
¼ teaspoon ground cloves
1 ½ cups orange juice

Preheat the oven to 350° F. In a large mixing bowl, lightly mix together the ham, pork, cracker crumbs, onion, mustard, milk and eggs. Form the mixture into 1½-inch balls and place them on a 10-inch pie plate. Bake for 30 minutes, turning occasionally. While the ham balls are cooking, combine the brown sugar, cornstarch, cloves and orange juice in a 2½-quart saucepan; cook over moderate heat, stirring constantly, until thickened. Reduce the heat and keep the sauce warm until the ham balls are cooked through. Drain the ham balls on paper towels, then add them to the sauce in the saucepan and simmer, covered, for 15 to 20 minutes or until the ham balls and sauce are hot and the flavors have had a chance to blend.

Eight main-course servings.

❧ LEG OF LAMB WITH ROSEMARY

Don't follow the instructions on most meat thermometers or your lamb will be overcooked. All you need is 165° F for well-done lamb, or if you prefer it a little pink, 140 to 150° will do. (I prefer lamb at about 140 to 145°.) If there's time, season the lamb for a few hours before cooking so that it can absorb the garlic and rosemary flavors.

One 4- to 5-pound leg of lamb
3 large cloves garlic, cut into
  slivers
Rosemary (fresh if possible)
Salt
Freshly ground pepper
3 to 4 slices bacon
Vinegar

Preheat the oven to 350° F. Trim the excess fat from the lamb and, using the tip of a sharp knife, cut slits all over it, the more the better. Fill the slits with garlic slivers and bits of rosemary. Rub the roast with salt and pepper. Place the bacon in the bottom of a roasting pan, add the lamb, fat side *up.* Bake, basting from time to time with a few tablespoons of vinegar, 20 to 25 minutes per pound, or until a meat thermometer registers 140 to 150° F for rare to medium, 165° for well done.

Six servings.

❧ LAMB CREPES ORIENTAL

An elegant use for leftover lamb.

1 onion, chopped fine
3 tablespoons butter
2 cups chopped cooked lamb
¼ cup lamb gravy or beef broth
1 small head lettuce, shredded
Freshly ground pepper
8 crepes (p. 64)

ORIENTAL SAUCE:

  1 tablespoon cornstarch
  2 tablespoons soy sauce
  ½ teaspoon powdered ginger
  1 tablespoon sherry
  1 cup lamb gravy or beef
    broth

Sauté the onion in the butter until golden, then add the lamb and the ¼ cup gravy or broth and simmer until the lamb is heated through. Add the lettuce and cook briefly *just until the lettuce wilts,* seasoning with pepper. Fill the crepes with the lamb mixture. Place the filled crepes, seam side *down,* in a heatproof serving dish.

Preheat the oven to 400° F. Combine the cornstarch, soy sauce, ginger and sherry in a small saucepan. Stir in the 1 cup gravy or broth and cook over moderate heat until thick. Spoon the sauce over the filled crepes in the serving dish and place in the oven for about 10 minutes or until heated through.

Three to four servings.

❧ RAGOUT OF LAMB AND VEGETABLES

This is a good party dish to make ahead and freeze, especially if you use a baking dish that can go straight from the freezer to the oven and then to the table for serving.

3 pounds boneless stewing lamb, cut into 1½-inch cubes

6 tablespoons vegetable or corn oil

½ teaspoon freshly ground pepper

½ cup flour

2 cups beef broth

¼ cup sherry or white wine

2 cloves garlic, minced

24 small white onions

2 carrots, sliced thin

3 tablespoons fresh lemon juice

3 tablespoons chopped fresh parsley

Preheat the oven to 350° F. Dry the lamb with paper towels and brown the pieces in small batches in hot oil in a skillet. Place the meat in a 2½-quart baking dish or casserole with a cover. Mix the pepper and flour together and sprinkle the mixture over the lamb. Heat the broth, and add it, along with the sherry or wine and the garlic, to the baking dish. Cover and bake for 1 hour. Add the onions and carrots and cook for 45 minutes more or until the vegetables are done. Let stand for at least 10 minutes, then skim off the fat. Stir in the lemon juice and parsley before serving.

Six to eight servings.

❧ SHISH KEBAB

I frequently fall back on this dish, because everyone seems to like it, it's easy to double or triple and—best of all—it's quick, only needing attention during the 15 minutes before dinner. Serve it with Armenian Almond–Rice Pilaf (p. 81) and a green salad. Or, if there's room on the grill, thread vegetables—eggplant chunks, mushroom caps, green pepper slices, zucchini chunks, cherry tomatoes, parboiled white onions or whatever you like—on separate skewers and grill, basting with the marinade until lightly broiled. The vegetables will require less cooking than the meat.

MARINADE:

1 onion, minced
½ teaspoon Worcestershire sauce
½ cup red wine
¼ cup fresh lemon juice
¼ cup olive oil
2 cloves garlic, minced
Freshly ground pepper

2 pounds lamb (leg or shoulder),
*   cut into 1-inch cubes*

Mix all all marinade ingredients together in a 2-quart mixing bowl. Soak the lamb in the marinade for several hours or overnight. Stir from time to time. Thread the lamb onto skewers and brush with the marinade. Place under the broiler, or grill over charcoal, for 15 minutes or until done, basting and turning several times.

Four servings.

❧ VEAL WITH LEMON AND VEGETABLES

2 pounds stewing veal, cut in 1 ½-
inch cubes
½ cup flour
1 ½ tablespoons butter
4 small white onions, halved
2 carrots, cubed
½ cup white wine
1 teaspoon salt (or to taste)
Few slices of lemon peel
1 cup water
¼ pound fresh mushrooms,
sliced, then sautéed in butter
2 egg yolks
½ cup cream

Dredge the veal cubes in the flour. Sauté the veal in the butter in a 10-inch skillet until lightly browned. Add the onions, carrots, wine, salt, lemon peel and water. Simmer, covered, until the veal is tender, testing after 30 minutes. (It may take up to 1 hour, depending on the veal.) Add the sautéed mushrooms. In a small mixing bowl, beat together the egg yolks and cream. Gradually beat in a little hot liquid from the veal, then continue adding hot liquid until the egg yolk mixture is hot. Stir the egg yolk mixture into the stew. Heat, stirring, until the sauce is bubbly and slightly thickened. Do not boil.

Six servings.

❧ VEAL SCALLOPS IN MUSHROOM–TOMATO SAUCE

This is delicious and quick to make. It's expensive, too, but you can cut the cost by substituting turkey breast, cut into similar-sized pieces.

1 ½ pounds veal scallops (cut
from the leg)
Salt
Freshly ground pepper
Flour
4 tablespoons (½ stick) butter
½ pound fresh mushrooms, sliced
1 tablespoon finely chopped onion
½ cup chicken broth
¼ cup dry white wine
3 tablespoons Homemade Tomato
Sauce (p. 87) or 1 tablespoon
tomato paste
1 tablespoon chopped fresh
parsley

Preheat the oven to 350° F. Season the veal with salt and pepper and dip both sides into flour. Melt the butter in a 10-inch skillet and sauté the veal until browned on both sides. Transfer the veal to a 1½-quart baking dish. Using the same skillet, sauté the mushrooms lightly, then add the onion, broth and wine; cook briskly until the liquid is reduced by about half. Stir in the tomato sauce or paste. Pour over the veal and bake, covered for 30 minutes. Sprinkle with chopped parsley before serving.

Four servings.

SHRIMP-STUFFED TOMATOES WITH VARIATIONS

❧❧ GAZPACHO WITH YOGURT *and* QUICK SPINACH SOUP
❧❧ GUACAMOLE SALAD *and* CHICKEN-WALNUT PÂTÉ

🌼 VEAL WITH LEMON AND VEGETABLES

✤ SHISH KEBAB *and* HERBED ROAST BEEF WITH
OVEN-BROWNED POTATOES

✤ PARTY PORK ROAST WITH MUSHROOM STUFFING *and*
BOILED BEEF WITH VEGETABLES

 BEEF CURRY

POULTRY

❧ TARRAGON CHICKEN IN WHITE WINE

Simple to prepare, lovely to serve, this is one of my tried-and-true company and family dishes, always a success. To serve eight, use half again as much wine, lemon juice and oil, and double everything else.

¾ cup dry white wine
¼ cup fresh lemon juice
2 tablespoons olive oil
1 clove garlic, minced
Salt
1 broiler-fryer chicken (2 ½ to 3 pounds), cut up
Paprika
Freshly ground pepper
½ cup heavy cream
Dash of Worcestershire sauce
2 teaspoons fresh tarragon or 1 teaspoon dried

In roasting pan, combine the wine, lemon juice, oil, garlic and 1 teaspoon salt; blend well. Add the chicken pieces, turning to coat. Refrigerate, covered, for at least 3 hours, turning the chicken from time to time. Preheat the oven to 375° F. Sprinkle the chicken with paprika and pepper. Bake for 45 to 55 minutes or until fork-tender. Remove the chicken from the oven and reduce the oven temperature to 200° F.

Arrange the chicken on a platter and place it in the oven to keep warm while making the sauce. Reduce the pan juices to 1 ½ cups (3 cups if doubling the recipe). Add the cream and heat to the boiling point. Add the Worcestershire sauce and tarragon, taste and adjust the seasonings. Pour the sauce over the chicken and serve.

Four servings.

❧ MARION'S WALNUT CREEK CHICKEN

For those evenings when you're tired and don't feel like fussing, here's a wonderful recipe that's almost as easy as—and much nicer than—eating out. Serve it with rice. The leftover sauce is good over pork chops, too.

1 quart canned or Homemade
  Tomato Sauce (p. 87)
3 cloves garlic, minced
1 medium onion, chopped
½ teaspoon freshly ground
  pepper
Salt
2 bay leaves
1 teaspoon dried oregano,
  crumbled
½ teaspoon powdered cumin
¾ cup raisins
1 tablespoon vegetable or corn oil
1 tablespoon vinegar
3 to 4 pounds chicken, cut up

Preheat the oven to 350° F. Combine all the ingredients but the chicken in a 3-quart casserole with cover; stir to blend. Add the chicken and spoon the sauce over it. Cover and bake for 1½ hours.

Four to six servings.

❧ PARTY POULTRY

The best way to entertain is to have everyone eat in the kitchen. That way the cook isn't left out of the fun! This dish, with everything sliced and measured ahead of time, lets you cook while enjoying your company's company. Serve it over rice or noodles.

4 tablespoons (½ stick) butter
⅓ cup slivered, blanched
  almonds
1 ½ pounds boneless chicken or
  turkey breasts
½ sweet red pepper, sliced very
  thin
½ pound fresh mushrooms, sliced
1 cup chopped green onions,
  including the tops
1 package (10 ounces) frozen
  artichoke hearts, thawed
1 tablespoon flour
½ cup dry white wine or sherry
½ cup heavy cream
2 tablespoons Dijon-style mustard
¼ teaspoon freshly ground
  pepper
Salt
½ teaspoon dried dill
½ cup chopped fresh parsley

Melt the butter in a 10-inch skillet and sauté the almonds in it until golden; remove with a slotted spoon and set aside. Skin the chicken or turkey and cut it into ½-by-2-inch strips. Add the chicken to the remaining butter along with the red pepper, mushrooms, green onions and artichoke hearts. Stir over moderate heat for 3 minutes, tossing gently. Reduce the heat to low. Mix together the remaining ingredients and add them to the skillet, stirring gently. Cover and cook for 15 minutes over *very low* heat. Add the sautéed almonds and serve over rice or noodles.

Six servings.

✿ SESAME–SAGE CHICKEN

Use tarragon instead of sage to vary the flavor!

2 tablespoons sesame seeds
4 tablespoons (½ stick) butter, softened
1 teaspoon dried sage, crumbled
1 broiler chicken (about 4 pounds), split
1 tablespoon butter, melted
1 tablespoon olive oil

Preheat the oven to 450° F. Place the sesame seeds on a cookie sheet and brown them in the oven, shaking occasionally and watching carefully. Remove when lightly browned and reduce the oven heat to 350° F. Combine the softened butter with the sage. Using your fingers, carefully separate the skin of the chicken from the flesh, leaving it attached at one or two points. With a finger or spatula, spread the butter-sage mixture under the skin. Place the chicken, skin side up, in a 2-quart oblong baking dish. Combine the melted butter and the olive oil and brush the mixture on the chicken with a pastry brush. Sprinkle the browned sesame seeds over the chicken. Bake for 40 to 45 minutes or until the chicken is done.

Four servings.

✿ CHICKEN–WALNUT SAUTÉ

So good, and it takes less than 15 minutes to cook! Be sure to measure out all the ingredients before you start cooking. Of course, you may substitute slivered almonds for the walnuts. Serve with hot cooked rice.

2 whole chicken breasts
3 tablespoons vegetable or corn oil
3 to 4 green onions, chopped
2 medium stalks celery, chopped
1 tablespoon butter
¾ cup coarsely broken walnuts
1 teaspoon finely chopped lemon peel (yellow part only)
2 tablespoons soy sauce
1 tablespoon fresh lemon juice

Bone and skin the chicken breasts and cut them into bite-sized pieces. Heat the oil in a 10-inch skillet over moderate heat until sizzling hot. Add the chicken, green onion and celery and stir quickly until the chicken begins to brown. Add the butter, nuts and lemon peel. Continue to cook, uncovered, for a few minutes, stirring often. Turn off the heat; add the soy sauce and lemon juice and stir until the chicken is well coated with sauce. Serve at once with rice.

Four to six servings.

CHICKEN TERIYAKI SKEWERS

Another favorite, these are also good in small portions with cocktails. They're easily made up in the morning and left to marinate all day, but use wooden skewers if you do this.

3 whole chicken breasts
½ pound bacon
1 large green pepper, cut into
 1-inch squares
3 small navel oranges, cut into 8
 sections each
1 small pineapple, trimmed and
 cut into 1-inch cubes

MARINADE:

½ cup vegetable or corn oil
¼ cup soy sauce
Juice of 1 lemon
1 clove garlic, minced
3 to 4 tablespoons dry sherry
½ teaspoon powdered ginger

Bone and skin the chicken breasts and cut them into 1-inch cubes. Wrap each chicken piece in half a strip of bacon. Spear the chicken, pepper, oranges, and pineapple on heatproof skewers. Place the skewers in a shallow roaster. Mix all the marinade ingredients together and pour the mixture over the skewers. Marinate in the refrigerator, turning the skewers occasionally, for about 2 hours. Grill or broil, indoors or out, for about 10 minutes on each side or until the bacon is crisp. Heat the remaining marinade and spoon it over the skewers after they have been placed on a heatproof platter. Keep the platter hot in a 250° F oven for a few minutes until ready to serve.

Six servings.

⚜ CHICKEN CREPES

An elegant way to serve any leftovers, especially chicken.

12 crepes (use ½ recipe, see below)
4 tablespoons (½ stick) butter
2 tablespoons flour
2 cups milk
¼ teaspoon salt
Pinch of dry mustard
Freshly ground pepper
1 to 2 tablespoons sherry
½ pound fresh mushrooms, sliced
3 green onions, chopped fine
2 cups finely diced cooked chicken
¾ cup shredded Swiss cheese

Prepare the crepes and set them aside. Preheat the oven to 350° F. Melt *2 tablespoons* of the butter in a 1-quart saucepan, stir in the flour and cook over low heat, stirring constantly, for 3 or 4 minutes. Add the milk, stirring vigorously, and continue to stir until the sauce reaches the boiling point and thickens. Season with salt, dry mustard, pepper and sherry, tasting, until the sauce is lively and assertive. Set aside but keep warm. Melt the remaining *2 tablespoons* butter in a 10-inch skillet, add the mushrooms and green onions and sauté for about 5 minutes. Add the chicken and heat through. Stir the chicken-mushroom mixture into the sauce. Spoon the filling onto the crepes, roll them and place them side by side, seam side *down,* in a buttered broilerproof dish, about 8 by 11 by 2 inches. Sprinkle with Swiss cheese and put under the broiler until the crepes are heated through and the cheese is melted and lightly browned.

Four to six servings.

ALL-PURPOSE CREPES RECIPE

Stacked crepes freeze well, wrapped tightly in foil, but let them defrost completely to room temperature before you take them apart, or they may break. For other delicious crepe fillings, see Lamb Crepes Oriental (p. 53), Spinach Crepes (p. 125) and Peachy Crepes (p. 164).

1 cup flour
3 tablespoons butter, melted
3 eggs
⅔ cup milk
Pinch of salt
⅔ cup water
Melted butter or vegetable oil (for frying)

Blend the flour, butter, eggs, milk, salt and water in a blender or food processor. Refrigerate for about 1 hour before making the crepes. To make the crepes, put a 7-inch skillet over moderate heat and brush lightly with melted butter or oil. Add several table-spoonfuls of batter, then quickly tilt the pan so that the batter covers the bottom evenly in the thinnest possible layer; quickly pour any excess batter back into the bowl. Cook for just a few minutes or until the bottom of the crepe is lightly browned and the edges lift easily. Turn with a spatula (or lift by the edge with your fingers and flip over); brown lightly on the other side. Remove the finished crepe to a platter, brush the pan with more melted butter or oil and repeat.

Two dozen crepes.

❈ CHICKEN HASH

This is a frugal and easy party dish, especially when you have cooked chicken on hand. It's ideal for buffets, even brunch! I double the quantities for a big crowd and reduce them for everyday family eating. I like to put it all together in the morning, or even the night before, then pop it into the oven for 30 minutes when I get home.

4 cups cooked chicken (4 to 5 pounds)
4 cups chopped or thinly sliced celery
1 teaspoon salt
1 teaspoon dried tarragon, crumbled
¼ cup grated onion
1 tablespoon fresh lemon juice
1 cup sour cream
1 cup mayonnaise
¼ cup dry white wine or dry vermouth
1 cup blanched, sliced almonds, toasted
1 cup fresh bread crumbs
½ cup freshly grated Parmesan or Romano cheese

Cut the chicken into ¾-inch cubes. Thoroughly combine the chicken and celery with the salt, tarragon, onion, lemon juice, sour cream, mayonnaise, wine and almonds. Allow to stand for at least 1 hour. Preheat the oven to 350° F. Spoon the mixture into a buttered shallow 2-quart baking dish. (You may hold the dish in the refrigerator at this point until you're ready to bake it.) Top with the bread crumbs and cheese. Bake in the oven for 25 to 30 minutes or until heated through and lightly browned.

Six to eight servings.

Variation:

Try using Chicken Hash as a filling for crepes (p. 64).

❧ STUFFED TURKEY BREAST

2 pounds boned turkey breast
½ cup whole cranberry sauce
2 tablespoons butter, melted
2 tablespoons dry sherry
2 tablespoons grated orange peel
Salt
Freshly ground pepper

Preheat the oven to 450° F. Pound the turkey breast with a wooden hammer or the flat side of a cleaver until flattened, then cut it into 4 equal pieces. Spread cranberry sauce over each piece, roll and pin it together with a toothpick. Brush melted butter on the surface of the rolls. Arrange them in a baking dish and place them in the oven. Reduce the oven temperature to 375° F and bake for 15 minutes. Drizzle them with dry sherry, then sprinkle them with grated orange peel. Bake for an additional 10 minutes. Serve them warm, seasoned with salt and pepper to taste.

Four servings.

❧ CORNISH HENS WITH WILD RICE

One of my favorites for a simple and elegant candlelit supper, yet easy and inexpensive for a family meal.

1 package (6 ounces) mixed
*   long-grain and wild rice*
1 ¼ cups water
4 tablespoons (½ stick) butter
1 medium onion, chopped fine
1 tablespoon flour
2 cups chicken broth
1 package (10 ounces) frozen
*   green peas, thawed*
2 Cornish hens (about 1 pound
*   each), halved*
Butter
Salt
Freshly ground pepper
Dry mustard

Preheat the oven to 325° F. Combine the rice (discard the packaged seasonings) and water in a 2-quart saucepan. Cover and cook for 12 minutes or just until the water is absorbed. Melt the butter in a 3-quart casserole over moderate heat. Add the onion and cook for 3 minutes. Sprinkle in the flour, stirring to combine. Gradually add the broth and heat to the boiling point. Stir in the rice and peas gently but thoroughly. Rub the hen pieces with butter, salt, pepper and mustard. Arrange them on the rice mixture; cover and bake for 45 minutes or until the rice is done and the hen pieces are fork-tender.

Four servings.

❧ CHICKEN OR TURKEY CROQUETTES

I like this old-fashioned dish so much that I poach chicken breasts just to make it. But it's really a good way to use those yummy leftovers! (For more suggestions, see Using Leftovers, p. 180.)

4 tablespoons (½ stick) butter
1 small onion, chopped very fine
¼ cup flour
1 cup milk
Salt
Pepper
Pinch of nutmeg
1 to 2 drops hot pepper sauce
4 cups finely chopped cooked
    chicken or turkey
Fine bread crumbs
3 eggs, beaten with 1 tablespoon
    water
Butter and oil (for frying)
Leftover gravy or tomato sauce

Melt the butter in a 10-inch skillet, add the onion and cook over low heat until soft. Add the flour and stir over low heat for 3 to 4 minutes. Gradually add the milk, stirring constantly, and cook over moderate heat until the sauce reaches the boiling point and thickens. Season with salt, pepper, nutmeg and pepper sauce until peppy. Mix this sauce with the chopped chicken or turkey and refrigerate. Once the mixture has chilled, form it into patties and roll them first in fine bread crumbs, then in beaten egg, and then again in fine bread crumbs. Refrigerate until ready to cook. Fry on both sides in a mixture of butter and oil until browned. Serve with gravy or tomato sauce.

Six to eight servings.

Variations:

Substitute a chopped fresh herb or some mild curry powder for the nutmeg.

CHICKEN LIVERS SAUTÉ

Serve this with white or brown rice, moistened with a bit of soy sauce—an unbeatable combination! Or serve over Herb Biscuits (p. 145).

2 tablespoons butter
1 small onion, chopped
¼ pound fresh mushrooms, sliced
1 pound chicken livers
¼ cup sherry
1 small apple, peeled, cored and
* chopped*
Salt
Freshly ground pepper
½ cup sour cream

Melt the butter in a 10-inch skillet. Sauté the onion and mushrooms until the onion is soft. Trim the livers and cut each in half. Add them to the skillet and cook over low heat, stirring, for about 3 minutes. Add the sherry, apple, salt and pepper. Cook until the apples are tender, about 2 minutes. Remove the skillet from the heat and add the sour cream. Mix and toss everything lightly over heat until just heated through. Do not boil.

Four servings.

FISH

❧ FISH WITH LEMON–HERB STUFFING

Of the several basic ways to prepare fish, I think stuffed fish is probably the most stylish. I like to leave the head and tail on the fish—it looks so dramatic when it's served.

1 whole red snapper, bass, pike, rockfish or lake trout (3 to 4 pounds)

LEMON–HERB STUFFING:

4 tablespoons (½ stick) butter
¼ cup chopped onion
¼ cup chopped celery
1 cup fresh bread crumbs
Peel of 1 lemon, grated (yellow part only)
1 tablespoon fresh lemon juice
¼ cup chopped fresh parsley
1 teaspoon fennel seed, crushed
Salt
Freshly ground pepper
Boiling water

Salt
Freshly ground pepper
Fresh lemon juice
4 tablespoons (½ stick) butter, melted
Dill sprigs
Lemon wedges

Clean the fish and prepare it for stuffing (removing the head and tail if you prefer).

To prepare the stuffing, melt the butter in a 1½-quart saucepan, then add the onion and celery and cook until soft. Add the bread crumbs, lemon peel, lemon juice, parsley and fennel seed. Season generously with salt and pepper and toss over low heat to combine. Add boiling water, 1 tablespoonful at a time, until the ingredients cling together, but are not at all soggy.

Preheat the oven to 400° F. Sprinkle the fish lightly inside and out with salt, pepper and lemon juice. Fill the cavity with Lemon–Herb Stuffing. Bind the fish with soft string to close the cavity and hold its shape. Place the fish in a roasting pan. Brush with some of the melted butter, then pour the remaining butter over the fish. Bake, allowing 10 to 12 minutes per pound; baste several times with the pan juices. Remove the string. Garnish with dill sprigs and lemon wedges and serve at once.

Four to six servings.

Variation:

Use the stuffing to make fish roll-ups, spreading it down the center of a firm, white fish fillet. Roll the fillet up, starting with the narrow end. Fasten with a toothpick, drizzle with butter and bake.

❧ FISH FILLETS WITH SPINACH

Fish and spinach have a very special affinity for each other. I use this recipe to add some zip to bland or frozen fish.

2 tablespoons butter
2 tablespoons chopped onion
Salt
Freshly ground pepper
4 sole, scrod, whitefish or other
  fish fillets (about 1 ¼ pounds)
½ cup dry white wine
1 pound fresh spinach or 2
  packages (10 ounces each)
  frozen

SAUCE:

  2 tablespoons butter
  2 tablespoons flour
  ⅔ cup milk
  ⅓ to ½ cup poaching liquid
    from fish
  Pinch of nutmeg
  ¼ teaspoon dry mustard
  Freshly ground pepper

3 to 4 tablespoons freshly grated
  Parmesan cheese
Lemon slices
Watercress or parsley sprigs

Preheat the oven to 200° F. Melt the butter in a 10-inch skillet, add the onion and sauté for just a minute, sprinkling with salt and pepper. Top the onion with the fish fillets and white wine, cover and poach just until the fish flakes easily. Meanwhile, wash the spinach and cook it quickly in a saucepan, using only the water that sticks to the leaves; do not overcook. (If you're using frozen spinach, cook it briefly and squeeze it dry.) Drain the spinach and arrange it on an ovenproof platter. Carefully lift the fillets and arrange them on top of the spinach; save ½ cup of the poaching liquid. Keep the platter warm in the oven while making the sauce.

To make the sauce, melt the butter in a small saucepan, add the flour and cook over low heat, stirring constantly, for 3 to 4 minutes. Gradually add the milk and ⅓ cup of the poaching liquid, stirring vigorously. Cook until the sauce reaches the boiling point and thickens. Add the remaining liquid if it seems necessary. Season with the nutmeg, mustard and pepper.

Spoon the sauce over the fish and sprinkle with the cheese. Turn the oven up to 425° F and bake for 10 to 15 minutes or until well heated. Garnish with lemon slices and watercress or parsley and serve.

Four servings.

❧ FRIED FISH WITH SOUR CREAM SAUCE

We've all had fried fish, of course. But the sour cream sauce makes it into another kind of feast altogether.

SOUR CREAM SAUCE:

¾ cup sour cream
1 tablespoon fresh lemon juice
1 ½ tablespoons chopped fresh parsley
3 tablespoons finely chopped green onions, including the tops

¾ cup flour
½ teaspoon salt
¾ teaspoon paprika
½ teaspoon freshly ground pepper
4 fish fillets (about 1 pound)
2 eggs, lightly beaten
2 tablespoons butter
Chopped chives or chopped fresh parsley
Lemon wedges

Mix all the sauce ingredients together and set aside in the refrigerator.

Mix together the flour, salt, paprika and pepper. Dip the fish into this mixture, then into the eggs, then into the flour mixture again. Refrigerate the coated fish for 30 to 45 minutes. In a 10-inch skillet, fry the fish in the butter for 5 to 10 minutes, turning once, until the fish is cooked and each side is crisp and lightly browned. Serve immediately, topped with the sauce. Garnish with chives or parsley and lemon wedges.

Four servings.

❧ BAKED FISH AND VEGETABLE DINNER

3 large potatoes, peeled and sliced thin
Salt
½ pound fresh mushrooms, sliced
1 pound zucchini, cut into ⅛-inch slices
4 large tomatoes, peeled, seeded and sliced
2 green onions, sliced thin
1 ½ pounds fish fillets (haddock, perch, scrod, flounder or sole)
2 tablespoons butter, melted
1 teaspoon chopped fresh thyme or ½ teaspoon dried
1 teaspoon chopped fresh basil or ½ teaspoon dried
Freshly ground pepper
Lemon slices

Preheat the oven to 350° F. Generously butter a 2-quart baking dish. Arrange the potatoes in the dish and sprinkle lightly with salt. Cover with foil and bake for 15 minutes. Uncover and place the mushrooms, zucchini, tomatoes and green onions over the partially cooked potatoes. Place the fish fillets over the vegetables, and cut a few diagonal slashes in the fish. Dribble the melted butter over the fish and sprinkle with the herbs, salt and pepper. Bake, uncovered, until the fish is slightly browned and flakes easily. This may take from 10 to 20 minutes, depending on the thickness of the fillets. Do not overcook. Garnish with lemon slices.

Four to six servings.

❧ FISH FILLETS AU GRATIN

2 tablespoons fine cracker crumbs
1 pound perch, flounder or other fish fillets
1 cup canned tomatoes with liquid
2 tablespoons chopped onion
¼ teaspoon salt
Freshly ground pepper
1 tablespoon butter
¼ cup shredded Cheddar cheese

Preheat the oven to 375° F. Sprinkle a lightly greased, broilerproof 2-quart baking dish with the crumbs; arrange the fish on the crumbs. Combine the tomatoes, onion, salt and pepper and pour over the fish, then dot with butter. Bake for about 20 minutes or until the fish flakes easily and is opaque. Sprinkle with cheese and return to the oven until the cheese melts, about 5 minutes, or place under the broiler until the cheese is lightly browned.

Four servings.

Variations:

Add fresh herbs—dill, chervil, oregano—to the tomato mixture. And use different cheeses—shredded mozzarella, Gruyère or Swiss work well.

❧ FISH VINAIGRETTE

This tastes even better after a day or two in the refrigerator. A good summer dinner or lunch, it also makes a nice appetizer—served in small portions, of course.

1 ½ pounds fillets of flounder, haddock or sole
About ½ cup flour
4 to 5 tablespoons butter

VINAIGRETTE DRESSING:

¼ cup fresh lemon juice
Peel of 1 lemon, grated (yellow part only)
½ teaspoon salt
Dash of hot pepper sauce
1 clove garlic, minced
½ cup vegetable or corn oil

GARNISHES:

Sliced green onion
Carrot curls or grated carrots
Chopped fresh parsley
Black or green olives
Lemon wedges

Dip the fish fillets into the flour, then sauté them in a 10-inch skillet in butter, turning once, until the fish flakes easily with a fork and is opaque; do not over-cook. Carefully remove them to a serving platter. Mix the vinaigrette dressing ingredients together and pour this over the fish. Refrigerate for at least 6 hours. Before serving, garnish the platter with all, or any combination of, the suggested garnishes.

Four main-course servings.

❧ POACHED SALMON WITH DILL SAUCE

Make this when salmon is in season—it will be fresher and cheaper. It's an easy, elegant meal. I serve it hot or at room temperature, depending on the weather and my mood.

COURT BOUILLON:

1 carrot, sliced
1 onion, sliced
1 stalk celery, sliced
1 large lemon, sliced
1 bay leaf
4 black peppercorns, slightly crushed
2 sprigs fresh parsley
2 teaspoons salt
3 cups water

6 small salmon steaks (about 1 inch thick)

SAUCE:

1 cup mayonnaise
1 teaspoon Dijon-style mustard
2 tablespoons chopped fresh dill or 2 teaspoons dried
1 tablespoon fresh lemon juice

Mix together the ingredients for the court bouillon and, in a 10-inch skillet, bring to a boil. Reduce the heat and simmer, covered, for about 30 minutes. Remove the vegetables and lemon with a slotted spoon. Cook the salmon steaks gently in the bouillon, covered, for about 8 to 10 minutes or until the fish flakes easily with a fork. Meanwhile, combine all the ingredients for the sauce in a serving bowl. When the fish is done, remove it carefully and serve it either hot or at room temperature, with the sauce spooned on the side.

Six servings.

❧ GRILLED SWORDFISH WITH HORSERADISH SAUCE

Swordfish is expensive. I save it for special summer evenings.

MARINADE:

¾ cup dry white wine
¼ cup fresh lemon juice
Salt
Freshly ground pepper
½ teaspoon dry mustard
1 tablespoon chopped fresh dill
  or 1 teaspoon dried

4 small swordfish steaks (about
¾ inch thick)

HORSERADISH SAUCE:

¾ cup sour cream
¼ cup mayonnaise
2 to 3 tablespoons prepared
  horseradish
½ teaspoon prepared mustard
1 tablespoon fresh lemon juice

Mix the marinade ingredients together in a shallow pan and add the swordfish, turning the fish once or twice and marinating for at least 1 hour. Meanwhile combine the ingredients for Horseradish Sauce in a serving bowl. When the fish has finished marinating, remove it, but save the marinade.

Prepare an outdoor charcoal fire. Brush the fish steaks with the reserved marinade and broil them over hot coals for about 5 minutes. Turn the steaks and brush again. Cook for 5 to 7 minutes longer or until the fish flakes easily. Remove to a serving platter. Serve with Horseradish Sauce.

Four servings.

❧ SHERRIED SHRIMP

1 ½ pounds fresh or frozen
shrimp
4 tablespoons (½ stick) butter
5 cloves garlic, minced
2 tablespoons fresh lemon juice
Freshly ground pepper
¾ cup dry sherry
2 tablespoons chopped fresh
  parsley
2 tablespoons chopped fresh chives
  or green onions
Salt
Lemon wedges

If you are using fresh shrimp, shell and devein it; if frozen, thaw it. Melt the butter in a shallow 2½-quart casserole over moderate heat. Add the garlic, shrimp, lemon juice and pepper. Cook, stirring, until the shrimp turn pink, about 5 minutes. Add the sherry, parsley and chives. Taste, add salt cautiously, and bring just to a boil. Serve at once with lemon wedges.

Four servings.

❧ SHELLFISH RAMEKINS

I sometimes serve this as an appetizer, using smaller portions and spooning the mixture into tiny ramekins.

1 cup chopped fresh clams, with liquid, or 1 can (6 ½ ounces) minced clams, with liquid
⅓ cup dry white wine
1 pound sea or bay scallops
1 cup half-and-half or light cream
2 tablespoons butter
2 tablespoons flour
2 egg yolks, well beaten
6 tablespoons freshly grated Parmesan cheese
½ pound small shrimp, shelled
½ cup fresh bread crumbs

Preheat the oven to 350° F. Drain the juice from the fresh or canned clams into a 2-quart saucepan. Add the wine and scallops, cover and cook over low heat until the scallops turn white, about 2 to 3 minutes. Remove the scallops with a slotted spoon and reserve. Measure the cooking liquid: There should be ¾ cup; if more, reduce by pouring the liquid back into the saucepan and boiling. Now add the half-and-half or light cream and warm this liquid over low heat. In another 2-quart saucepan, melt the butter. Blend in the flour and cook, stirring constantly, for 3 to 4 minutes. Gradually add the half-and-half mixture and cook, stirring constantly, until the sauce reaches the boiling point and thickens. Beat about *½ cup* of the hot sauce into the egg yolks, then pour this back into the saucepan. Add *4 tablespoons* of the cheese and cook for 2 minutes. Remove from the heat; gently stir in the clams, scallops and shrimp. Spoon the mixture into 4 buttered 10-ounce ovenproof dishes. Mix the remaining *2 tablespoons* cheese with breadcrumbs and sprinkle over each dish. Bake for about 15 minutes or until the shrimp is pink and the mixture is bubbling hot.

Four main-course servings.

RICE, BEANS, GRAINS *and* PASTA

❧ PERFECT FLUFFY BUTTERED RICE

This dish is light and delicious. I find it fits beautifully into my cooking schedule if I start it 40 minutes before my roast or casserole finishes cooking.

1 cup chicken broth
1 ¼ cups water
1 cup uncooked long-grain rice
½ teaspoon salt
½ teaspoon fresh lemon juice
2 to 3 tablespoons butter, melted

Preheat the oven to 350° F. Combine the chicken broth and water in a 2-quart ovenproof saucepan and bring to a boil. Add the rice, salt and lemon juice and return to a boil. Remove from the heat. Cover and bake in the oven for 25 to 30 minutes or until the rice is tender. Fluff the rice with a fork, pour the butter over it and serve immediately.

Four servings.

❧ ARMENIAN ALMOND–RICE PILAF

To toast chopped almonds (or any other kind of nut), spread them on a cookie sheet in a 375° F oven, or put them in a toaster-oven if you have one. Stir once or twice and watch carefully to see that they don't burn—5 minutes should be enough!

1 tablespoon vegetable or corn oil
½ cup very fine egg noodles
1 cup uncooked long-grain rice
Salt
Freshly ground pepper
4 tablespoons (½ stick) butter
2 cups chicken broth, heated
½ cup finely chopped almonds, toasted

Heat the oil in a 10-inch skillet and cook the noodles in it over moderate heat, stirring gently, until lightly browned. Add the rice, stirring to coat, then add the salt, pepper, butter and broth, stirring until the butter melts. Cover and cook over very low heat, without stirring, for 25 to 30 minutes or until all the liquid is absorbed. Let stand, uncovered, for 5 minutes, then stir in the almonds, fluff and serve.

Four to six servings.

❧ ZUCCHINI RISOTTO

The secret to a good risotto is long, slow cooking and constant attention. But it pays off; I rarely have leftovers. You can also make this dish with leftover cooked zucchini: Just dice and heat the zucchini and add it to the rice when it is done, along with the cheese.

3 tablespoons vegetable or corn oil
2 green onions, chopped
1 clove garlic, halved
3 small zucchini, shredded
1 teaspoon chopped fresh basil or ½ teaspoon dried
Salt
Freshly ground pepper
Dash of hot pepper sauce
About 2 tablespoons butter
1 cup uncooked rice
2 cups chicken broth, heated to the boiling point
¼ cup freshly grated Parmesan or Romano cheese

Heat the oil in a 10-inch skillet. Add the green onions and garlic and cook until the onions are soft. Add the zucchini and cook over low heat until tender (2 to 3 minutes should do it), sprinkling with basil, salt, pepper and pepper sauce as it cooks. Remove from the skillet and set aside. Melt enough butter to cover the bottom of the skillet, then add the rice, stirring until well coated. Gradually add *¼ cup* of the boiling chicken broth and cook over low heat, stirring constantly, as the rice absorbs the liquid. Continue adding the hot broth, *¼ cup* at a time, waiting until the previous addition is completely absorbed before adding more liquid. Keep the broth at the boiling point, and stir constantly to prevent sticking. If you run out of chicken broth, use boiling water to finish. Sample the rice, and when it is tender, stir in the cooked zucchini and the cheese. Serve at once.

Six servings.

❧ BROWN RICE WITH MUSHROOMS

½ cup (1 stick) butter
1 cup uncooked brown rice
1 can (10 ½ ounces) condensed beef broth
1 cup water
½ pound fresh mushrooms, sliced
1 small onion, minced

Preheat the oven to 325° F. Melt *4 tablespoons* of the butter in a 3-quart casserole over moderate heat. Add the rice and cook, stirring constantly, for 3 or 4 minutes; do not brown. Add the broth and water. Cover and bake in the oven for 50 minutes. Meanwhile, melt the remaining *4 tablespoons* butter in a small skillet. Sauté the mushrooms and onion in it over low heat for

5 minutes. Remove the casserole from the oven. Stir in the mushrooms, onions and butter. Cover; return to the oven and bake for 30 to 35 minutes longer or until the rice is tender. Fluff with a fork and serve.

Six servings.

❧ HERBED OLIVE RICE

This colorful, peppy rice dish is ideal with plain broiled fish. It's a good way to use leftover cooked rice and can also be served cold as a rice salad if you add a little lemon juice and some olive oil.

2 cups firm cooked rice
¾ cup chopped pimiento-stuffed
    green olives
4 anchovy fillets, chopped
3 tablespoons finely chopped
    onion
¼ cup chopped fresh parsley
1 teaspoon chopped fresh
    marjoram or thyme or ½
    teaspoon dried
1 tablespoon drained, chopped
    capers
Freshly ground pepper
3 medium ripe tomatoes, peeled,
    seeded and chopped coarse

Preheat the oven to 350° F. Butter a 2-quart casserole. Add to the casserole, mixing well, the rice, olives, anchovies, onion, herbs, capers and pepper. Add the tomatoes, stirring gently to distribute. Cover and bake for 15 minutes or until heated through.

Four to six servings.

o᲎᪾o EMMY'S COUNTRY BEAN POT

Use a 4- to 5-quart pot for these.

2 cups uncooked pea beans
⅓ cup diced salt pork
1 tablespoon vegetable or corn oil
2 carrots, shredded
2 large onions, chopped
2 quarts water
1 large hambone
1 ½ cups chopped celery
3 cups finely chopped cabbage
1 clove garlic, minced
1 teaspoon crumbled dried sage
1 bay leaf
2 tablespoons tomato paste
1 tablespoon dark molasses
½ teaspoon freshly ground
   pepper
Salt

Soak the beans overnight. Next day sauté the salt pork in the oil. Add the carrots and onions and sauté for about 2 minutes. Add the water and the remaining ingredients. Simmer for about 2 hours or until the beans are tender.

Six to eight servings.

❧ BACON–BEAN BAKE

This recipe has been a favorite at Corning for years. It's an easy bean pot, made with lots of bacon and canned beans. (Beans are one of the few canned items I use. I always keep them on hand for emergencies.)

10 slices bacon, cut into 1-inch pieces
1 cup chopped onion
2 cans (15 ounces each) lima beans, drained, liquid reserved
2 cans (15 ounces each) red kidney beans, drained, liquid reserved
1 cup canned or Homemade Tomato Sauce (p. 87)
¼ cup molasses
2 tablespoons vinegar
1 teaspoon dry mustard

Preheat the oven to 350° F. Cook the bacon in a 3-quart saucepan over moderate heat until crisp. Remove the bacon and pour off all but 2 tablespoons of the bacon fat. Add the onion and cook over low heat until limp but not browned. Remove from the heat. Blend the bean liquids; measure out 1 cup and stir the liquid into the onions along with the tomato sauce, molasses, vinegar and mustard. Add the cooked bacon and the beans and stir well. Cover and bake for 40 to 45 minutes or until the liquid is bubbling and somewhat reduced and thickened.

Six servings.

❧ BARLEY CASSEROLE

More people ought to know that barley does not just belong in soups. I find its nutlike flavor so appealing that I serve it often as a base for creamed chicken or turkey or as a side dish with duck or pork. I sometimes add chopped peeled apple when serving it with the latter.

¼ cup finely chopped onion
¼ cup finely chopped carrot
¼ cup finely chopped celery
2 to 3 tablespoons butter
1 cup medium pearl barley (not the quick-cooking variety!)
2 cups beef or chicken broth
1 ½ cups water
Salt
Freshly ground pepper
Chopped fresh parsley

Preheat the oven to 300° F. In a 2½-quart casserole, sauté the onion, carrot and celery in the butter. Add the barley, broth and water. Cover and bake for about 1½ hours, adding a little more water or broth if necessary, until the barley is tender. Let stand for 15 minutes or until all the liquid is absorbed. Season with salt and pepper and sprinkle with lots of parsley.

Six to eight servings.

❧ BULGUR PILAF

This is one of my standbys. It can be tossed together with ease and lends itself to innumerable variations. Mushrooms are good in it, and when I'm serving it with lamb, I add 2 or 3 finely chopped tablespoonfuls of the mint that is threatening to take over my lawn!

1 ½ cups uncooked bulgur
2 cups chicken broth
½ cup finely chopped onion
1 stalk celery, chopped fine
2 tablespoons butter
Juice of 1 lemon (about 2 tablespoons)
¼ cup chopped fresh parsley
Salt
Freshly ground pepper

Preheat the oven to 350° F. Soak the bulgur in the broth for about 15 minutes. Sauté the onion and celery in the butter in a 2-quart casserole until soft but not browned. Add the bulgur-broth mixture, lemon juice, parsley, salt and pepper and stir well. Cover and bake for about 30 minutes.

Four to six servings.

❧ SUPER-EASY BACON AND RAISIN POLENTA

This polenta is good with melted butter, cheese, gravy or tomato sauce poured over it. Served with eggs, it makes a wonderful breakfast or brunch. Leftover polenta can be fried, broiled or baked.

4 to 6 slices bacon
1 ½ quarts water
2 cups yellow cornmeal
1 teaspoon salt
½ cup raisins or currants

Fry the bacon, drain thoroughly and crumble; set aside. Bring the water to a boil in a 2½-quart saucepan. Reduce the heat to low and pour in the cornmeal in a thin stream, stirring constantly with a wooden spoon. When all the cornmeal is stirred into the water, add the salt. Stir for about 10 minutes or until the mixture is so thick that the spoon will stand up in it. Add the raisins and bacon and mix thoroughly. Serve at once.

Six to eight servings.

HOMEMADE TOMATO SAUCE (FOR PASTA AND EVERYTHING ELSE)

Here's a basic tomato sauce that can be made with either fresh or canned tomatoes. It freezes well and is always great to have on hand. This sauce can be varied by the addition of meat, vegetables, spices and other ingredients. One pint is enough for about 1 pound of pasta (or 4 good servings). This sauce is also good in many other kinds of dishes and is called for in recipes throughout this book. To peel tomatoes, submerge them in boiling water for 30 seconds or so, then remove the skins with a sharp knife.

3 tablespoons olive or vegetable oil
1 large onion, sliced thin
2 cloves garlic, minced
1 cup chopped green pepper (optional)
1 cup sliced fresh mushrooms (optional)
3 pounds ripe tomatoes, peeled and quartered, or 3 cans (16 ounces each) tomatoes, chopped, with liquid
Salt
Freshly ground pepper
2 teaspoons chopped fresh basil or 1 teaspoon dried
2 teaspoons chopped fresh marjoram or oregano or 1 teaspoon dried
1 small carrot, grated
About 3 tablespoons tomato paste

Heat the oil in a 3-quart saucepan, then add the onion and garlic (and green pepper if you're using it) and sauté over medium-low heat until the onion is transparent, not browned. (Add the mushrooms now, if you wish, and sauté them for just a minute or two longer.) Add the tomatoes and simmer over low heat, stirring from time to time to prevent sticking, until the sauce thickens and the tomatoes lose their shape, about 1 hour. When the sauce has cooked for a while, begin to season it with salt, pepper, basil and marjoram or oregano. When the sauce is ready, taste and adjust the seasonings, adding the grated carrot for a touch of sweetness, and some tomato paste if the sauce lacks strong color or thickness. Cook a bit longer until the new seasonings are thoroughly absorbed. You can puree this sauce in a blender or food processor, but I prefer a chunky texture.

Two-and-a-half to three pints.

❖ CLASSIC MEATBALLS AND SPAGHETTI

There are so many unusual sauces for pasta, but I still like this "old-fashioned" approach. Adding green olives to these meatballs is a nice touch. Sometimes I change them completely by using raisins instead.

SAUCE:

2 cloves garlic, minced
3 tablespoons olive oil
1 large, or 2 small, pork chops
  (about ½ pound)
3 cans (1 pound each)
  tomatoes, chopped, with
  liquid, or 6 cups peeled,
  chopped fresh tomatoes
1 can (12 ounces) tomato
  paste
1 tablespoon chopped fresh
  basil or 1 teaspoon dried
Salt
Freshly ground pepper

MEATBALLS:

1 pound ground beef
1 egg
¼ cup soft bread crumbs
¼ cup chopped fresh parsley
¼ cup sliced pitted green
  olives or raisins
¼ cup freshly grated
  Parmesan cheese

Oil (for frying)
1 pound uncooked spaghetti
Freshly grated Parmesan cheese

Begin with the sauce, which takes a bit of cooking. Sauté the garlic briefly in the olive oil (do not brown), then add the pork chops and brown on both sides. Remove and drain on paper towels. Cut the meat into ½-inch pieces. Return to the pot. Add the tomatoes, tomato paste, basil, salt and pepper, reduce the heat and cook, uncovered, for about 3 hours, stirring from to time to prevent sticking.

While the sauce is cooking, prepare the meatballs by combining all the ingredients lightly and forming this mixture into small balls. Brown the meatballs either in a skillet in enough oil to just film the bottom of the pan or in a baking pan in a 400° F oven, turning occasionally. Add the meatballs to the sauce for the last 30 minutes or so of cooking. Cook the spaghetti until tender but still firm when you bite it (*al dente,* as the Italians say). Drain and serve, topped with meatballs and sauce. Pass freshly grated Parmesan cheese on the side.

Four to six servings.

Variation:

Make pork meatballs by substituting for the ground beef ¼ pound crumbled sweet Italian sausage mixed with ¾ pound ground pork. Omit the pork chops from the sauce and brown ½ pound hot Italian sausages instead.

❀ CORNISH HENS WITH WILD RICE

CHICKEN TERIYAKI SKEWERS *and* CHICKEN-WALNUT SAUTÉ

FISH WITH LEMON-HERB STUFFING

(L to R)
FISH FILLETS WITH SPINACH, SALMON WITH DILL SAUCE,

FISH VINAIGRETTE *and* FISH FILLETS AU GRATIN

❧ VEGETABLE FETTUCCINE

🌸 EMMY'S COUNTRY BEAN POT

❧ PASTA AND CLAMS

Delicate and delicious.

4 tablespoons (½ stick) butter
2 cloves garlic, minced
1 ½ teaspoons prepared
*   horseradish*
1 quart fresh clams, shucked and
*   drained, liquid reserved*
1 can (6 ounces) tomato paste
2 tablespoons dry white wine
1 pound uncooked thin spaghetti
¼ cup chopped fresh parsley
Freshly ground pepper

Heat the butter in a 10-inch skillet. Add the garlic, horseradish and clams and sauté for 1 minute. Stir in the tomato paste and cook, covered, for 1 minute. Add the clam liquid and wine and cook for 5 more minutes. Cook the spaghetti until tender but still firm when you bite into it; drain. Serve the sauce over the pasta and sprinkle with parsley and pepper.

Four servings.

❧ SPAGHETTI CARBONARA

Timing is the essential ingredient in making this easy pasta dish. The hot noodles cook the eggs and melt the cheese into a lovely rich sauce, but the mixing must be done quickly and thoroughly, and just before serving.

½ pound bacon or Canadian
*   bacon, chopped*
3 eggs
½ cup freshly grated Parmesan
*   cheese*
¼ cup heavy cream
1 pound uncooked thin spaghetti
Freshly ground black pepper
¼ cup chopped fresh parsley

Fry the bacon until you have lots of crispy bits. Drain on paper towels. In a 4-quart mixing bowl (large enough to hold all the pasta), beat the eggs and stir in the cheese and cream. Cook the spaghetti in boiling water until tender but still firm when you bite it. Drain quickly, then pour the spaghetti into the egg mixture. Toss rapidly for a minute or two or until creamy. Sprinkle with the bacon, pepper and parsley and serve at once.

Four servings.

Variation:

Sauté ¼ cup pine nuts and 1 finely chopped clove garlic in 2 tablespoons melted butter and toss with the spaghetti and the other ingredients.

❧ LINGUINE WITH TWO SAUCES

This is twice as nice as plain old pasta. It's rich and delicious, good as a main course with a green salad, or served with something very simple, such as broiled chicken.

TOMATO SAUCE:

2 tablespoons olive oil
2 cans (28 ounces each) tomatoes, chopped, with liquid
Salt
Freshly ground pepper
2 teaspoons chopped fresh basil or 1 teaspoon dried

BÉCHAMEL SAUCE:

4 tablespoons (½ stick) butter
½ cup flour
2 cups milk
1 cup grated Swiss cheese
½ cup dry white wine
Salt
Freshly ground pepper

1 pound uncooked linguine
½ cup freshly grated Romano cheese

In a 2½-quart saucepan, make the tomato sauce by heating the olive oil, then adding the remaining ingredients and cooking over low heat, stirring occasionally, until thickened, at least 45 minutes.

While the tomato sauce is cooking, make the béchamel sauce by melting the butter in a 1-quart saucepan. Add the flour and cook, stirring, for 3 to 4 minutes. Slowly add the milk and cook over moderate heat, stirring until it reaches the boiling point and thickens. Add the cheese and wine and season generously with pepper and a little salt. Put aside.

Preheat the oven to 350° F. Cook the pasta until just tender but firm when you bite it. Combine with the béchamel sauce and spread out in a buttered shallow 4-quart casserole. Cover with tomato sauce, sprinkle with grated Romano cheese and bake in the oven for 20 minutes.

Six servings.

VEGETABLE FETTUCCINE

Try whole-wheat pasta in this colorful, wholesome dish. The only secret: Be sure the vegetables are firm!

2 carrots, sliced very thin
2 small zucchini, sliced very thin
1 bunch broccoli, cut into small flowerettes with stems sliced very thin
1 pound uncooked fettuccine noodles
Salt
½ cup cream
Freshly grated Parmesan cheese
2 cloves garlic, minced
2 tablespoons butter
2 tablespoons vegetable or corn oil
½ pint cherry tomatoes, hulled
1 tablespoon chopped fresh basil or 1 teaspoon dried
Freshly ground pepper

Cook in separate pots the carrots, zucchini and broccoli until each is just tender, but still very crisp. (You can steam them over about an inch of boiling water in a covered saucepan or plunge them into a large pot of boiling water and cook briskly, uncovered, until just tender.) Set aside. Cook the noodles in salted boiling water until tender but still firm. While the noodles are cooking, heat the cream over low heat in a 1-quart saucepan and add the cheese, slowly stirring until melted. In a 10-inch skillet, sauté the garlic in the butter and oil for a few minutes. Add the tomatoes, basil and steamed vegetables, stirring until heated through. Season with salt and pepper. Drain the noodles. In a large serving bowl, toss the noodles with the cream and cheese mixture, top with the vegetable mixture and serve at once, passing around extra cheese and a pepper mill.

Four main-course servings.

◦❧◦ POLITICIANS' PASTA

Here's a happy combination of chicken and peas, a far cry from the standard fare on the politicians' dinner circuit.

2 chicken breasts, skinned, boned
*   and cut into ½-inch cubes*
½ cup sherry
4 tablespoons (½ stick) butter
2 cups frozen peas, thawed
1 cup heavy cream
1 ¼ cups freshly grated
*   Parmesan cheese*
Freshly ground pepper
1 pound uncooked fettuccine

Marinate the chicken in the sherry for about 15 minutes. In a 10-inch skillet, sauté the chicken in the butter until just done and slightly golden, about 8 to 10 minutes. Add the peas and heat through. Add the cream slowly, then fold in the grated cheese and pepper. Keep warm while the pasta cooks. Cook the fettuccine in boiling water until tender but still firm when you bite into it. Drain, then toss with the chicken mixture and serve at once.

Four servings.

◦❧◦ TURKEY TETRAZZINI

One of my favorite ways to serve leftover turkey. I sometimes sprinkle the top with toasted slivered almonds for an extra-special touch!

2 tablespoons butter
½ pound fresh mushrooms, sliced
*   thin*
3 tablespoons flour
1 ¼ cups chicken broth
½ cup light cream
¼ cup dry vermouth
Salt
Freshly ground pepper
2 cups diced cooked turkey
½ pound spaghetti, cooked and
*   drained*
½ cup freshly grated Parmesan
*   cheese*
Chopped fresh parsley

Preheat the oven to 350° F. Melt the butter in a 3-quart casserole over moderate heat; add the mushrooms and cook for 5 minutes. Add the flour, stirring with a whisk, and cook for 3 to 4 minutes, continuing to stir. Add the broth and cream slowly, stirring constantly. Continue stirring over low heat until the sauce reaches the boiling point and is slightly thickened. Add the vermouth and season with the salt and pepper until the flavor is good. Add the turkey and spaghetti to the sauce; toss gently until the spaghetti is well coated. Sprinkle with the cheese. Bake for 15 minutes or until heated through. Sprinkle with the parsley and serve.

Four servings.

⚜ SPINACH LASAGNA

I often serve this to my vegetarian friends. It's so good, it's almost made a vegetarian out of me!

2 *large bunches fresh spinach,*
 or
2 *packages (10 ounces each)*
 frozen leaf spinach, thawed
2 *tablespoons vegetable or corn oil*
1 *medium onion, chopped*
2 *cloves garlic, minced*
2 *cups canned or Homemade*
 Tomato Sauce (p. 87)
1 *can (6 ounces) tomato paste*
2 *teaspoons chopped fresh basil*
 or 1 teaspoon dried
1 ¼ *cups water*
Salt
Freshly ground pepper
2 *cups small-curd cottage cheese*
2 *eggs, lightly beaten*
10 *lasagna noodles, cooked and*
 drained
1 *cup shredded mozzarella cheese*
1 *cup freshly grated Parmesan*
 cheese

Preheat the oven to 350° F. If you are using fresh spinach, trim and wash it. Place the wet spinach in a saucepan, cover and cook just until soft; squeeze dry. Heat the oil in a 2½-quart casserole; add the onion and sauté until limp but not browned. Add the garlic and sauté for 2 minutes. Stir in the tomato sauce, tomato paste, basil and water. Season to taste with additional pepper and simmer for 20 minutes, stirring occasionally. Meanwhile, mix the cottage cheese and eggs; season with additional pepper. Arrange 5 of the cooked noodles to cover the bottom of a 13-by-9-by-1¾-inch baking dish. Spread the spinach, then the cottage cheese mixture over the noodles. Sprinkle with all the mozzarella cheese. Top with ½ the tomato sauce. Cover with the remaining noodles, then the remaining sauce. Sprinkle with the Parmesan cheese. Cover with foil and bake for 20 to 25 minutes.

Four servings.

❧ YANKEE DOODLE PIE

1 cup cream
1 cup diced white bread (about 2
  slices)
4 tablespoons (½ stick) butter
¾ cup cooked macaroni
½ cup diced sharp Cheddar
  cheese
1 tablespoon minced fresh parsley
½ green pepper, seeded and
  chopped
1 ounce pimiento, diced
¼ cup dry white wine
½ teaspoon Dijon-style mustard
3 eggs, beaten
Salt
Dash of cayenne
⅓ cup fine bread crumbs

Preheat the oven to 350° F. Scald the cream, then pour it over the diced bread. Melt *3 tablespoons* of the butter and add. Add the macaroni, cheese, parsley, green pepper and pimiento and stir. Add the wine and mustard to the beaten eggs and stir this mixture into the macaroni. Add salt to taste and the cayenne. Put the mixture into a well-buttered 1½-quart casserole, top with the bread crumbs and dot with the remaining *1 tablespoon* of butter. Bake until nicely browned, about 1 hour.

Four servings.

Variations:

• Add 1 cup shredded carrot to the ingredients.
• Top with 4 slices crumbled fried bacon.
• Line the bottom of the casserole with leftover ham.

❧ FRUITED NOODLE KUGEL

This sweetened noodle pudding is especially good with duck, and you can serve it as a dessert, too, topped with fruit-flavored yogurt.

¾ cup chopped dried apricots
1 cup boiling water
3 eggs
⅔ cup sugar
1 ¼ cups sour cream
½ cup raisins
½ teaspoon grated lemon peel
  (yellow part only)
⅛ teaspoon salt (or to taste)
½ pound medium egg noodles,
  cooked and drained

Preheat the oven to 350° F. In a medium mixing bowl, soak the apricots in the boiling water to soften. In a large electric mixer bowl or food processor, beat the eggs and sugar at high speed until thick and pale, 3 to 5 minutes. Add the sour cream and beat just until blended. Drain the apricots well, then add them to the egg mixture along with the raisins, lemon peel and salt. Stir lightly to combine. Fold in the noodles. Pour into a well-buttered 8-inch-square baking dish. Bake for 30 minutes or until set. Cut into squares and serve warm.

Four to six servings.

EGGS *and* EGG DISHES

❧ POACHED EGGS IN TOMATO SAUCE

Perfect for brunch, lunch or a midnight snack. Serve 1 egg per person as a stunning appetizer!

2 cups canned or Homemade Tomato Sauce (p. 87)
8 eggs
8 slices Italian bread or English muffin halves, toasted
¾ cup finely grated Swiss or Romano cheese
¼ cup chopped fresh parsley

Heat the sauce in a large skillet until bubbly. Break the eggs open and drop them gently into the sauce. Continue cooking, constantly spooning the sauce over the eggs until the whites are set. Remove the eggs with a slotted spoon, place each egg on a piece of toast and arrange on a platter. Cover with the sauce, sprinkle with the cheese and parsley and serve immediately.

Four servings.

Variation:

When serving as an appetizer, add chopped anchovies or tiny cooked shrimp to the sauce.

❧ BAKED EGGS IN MUSHROOM SAUCE

I often serve baked eggs for dinner, not just for brunch or lunch. They make a satisfying meal preceded by soup and followed by a salad and a light dessert.

3 slices bacon or ¼ cup minced ham
1 cup chopped fresh mushrooms
⅓ cup chopped onion
3 tablespoons butter
½ cup chicken broth
Salt
Freshly ground pepper
4 eggs
Freshly grated Parmesan or Swiss cheese or shredded mozzarella cheese

Preheat the oven to 350° F. If you are using bacon, sauté it until crisp; drain, crumble and set aside. In an 8½-inch skillet, sauté the mushrooms and onion in the butter for 2 minutes. Add the bacon or ham and chicken broth and cook for 3 minutes more, adding salt and pepper to taste. Divide the mixture among 4 well-buttered ramekins. Crack 1 large egg into each ramekin. Bake for 10–15 minutes or until the whites have set, adding grated cheese on top during the last 5 minutes of baking.

Four servings.

oᐧᔕᐧ SUPER SCRAMBLED EGGS

No need to wait for the cream cheese to soften if you have a food processor. Just put all the ingredients except the butter in the processor and blend for 1 minute or until smooth.

6 ounces cream cheese, softened
6 tablespoons light cream
2 tablespoons dry sherry
6 eggs, lightly beaten
¼ teaspoon salt (or to taste)
¼ teaspoon freshly ground
    pepper
2 tablespoons butter
Chopped fresh parsley

Combine the cream cheese, cream and sherry in a small mixing bowl. Add the eggs, beating until blended. Season lightly with salt and pepper. In an 8½-inch skillet, melt the butter over moderate heat. Pour mixture into the skillet. Cook, stirring frequently, over moderate heat for a very few minutes or just until the eggs are set as desired. Sprinkle with parsley and serve immediately.

Four to six servings.

oᐧᔕᐧ PUFFY BRUNCH OMELETTE

Rich but light, the soufflélike texture of this omelette makes it a lovely brunch or luncheon dish.

3 eggs, separated
¾ cup sour cream
1 ½ tablespoons thinly sliced
    green onions
1 ½ tablespoons chopped fresh
    parsley
½ cup finely diced ham or
    crumbled cooked sausage
¼ teaspoon freshly ground
    pepper (or to taste)
1 tablespoon butter
1 tablespoon chopped chives

In medium mixing bowl, beat the egg yolks until very thick. Beat ¼ cup of the sour cream into the yolks. Stir in the green onions, and the parsley, ham and pepper. In a separate small mixing bowl, beat the egg whites until stiff but not dry; fold this into the sour cream mixture. Melt the butter in an 8½-inch skillet over moderate heat, tilting so that the butter coats the bottom and sides. Pour in the egg mixture and smooth the surface gently. Reduce the heat to low and cook until the edges are set. Cover, and continue cooking over low heat for 10 to 15 minutes or until a knife inserted in the center comes out clean. Combine the chives and the remaining ½ cup sour cream and spread this over the omelette in a thin layer. Cut into quarters and serve.

Two servings.

❧ COTTAGE CHEESE PANCAKES

I like to serve these topped with sour cream or yogurt as a brunch or luncheon entrée. The raisins are optional, but make an excellent addition. Serve with bacon, sausage or grilled ham and add sautéed apples for a stunning flavor combination.

8 ounces creamed cottage cheese
2 eggs
Pinch of salt
3 tablespoons flour
¼ teaspoon powdered cinnamon
2 teaspoons granulated brown
  sugar
¼ cup raisins (optional)
Butter (for frying)

Preheat the oven to 200° F. Place the cottage cheese and eggs in the container of an electric blender or food processor. Process until smooth and foamy. Pour into a bowl and add the salt, flour, cinnamon and brown sugar. Add the raisins if desired. Place a 10-inch skillet over moderate heat and add just enough butter to film the bottom. When the butter begins to foam slightly, ladle the batter into the pan to make 2½-inch pancakes. Cook until the pancakes start to bubble. Flip them over and cook until lightly browned. Repeat with the remaining batter. Keep the cooked pancakes in the oven until ready to serve.

Three to four servings.

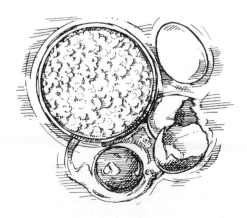

❧ About Frittatas

One of the most versatile dishes I've ever come across is the frittata, a kind of crustless quiche that's made on top of the stove and popped into the oven to finish. Be sure you have the proper pan—one that can go straight from stovetop to oven to broiler to table.

Here are some of my favorite frittata recipes; use them, but please try improvising as well, since this is a great dish for leftovers from the fridge.

Like a quiche, frittatas can be served either hot or at room temperature. They're good for lunch, brunch and cocktail snacks or as a first course at dinner. I love to serve frittatas at a picnic—they're just as good coming out of a basket as they are straight from the oven.

These recipes are for 8-egg frittatas, which serve 6. For 4 servings, use 6 eggs and an 8½-inch skillet, reducing the other ingredients slightly.

❧ BROCCOLI FRITTATA

1 pound trimmed broccoli, cooked but still crisp
¼ cup olive or vegetable oil
½ pound fresh mushrooms, sliced
2 cloves garlic, minced
Pinch of salt
¾ teaspoon freshly ground pepper
8 eggs, beaten
½ cup freshly grated Parmesan cheese

Preheat the oven to 350° F. Cut the broccoli into bite-sized pieces. Heat the oil in a 10-inch skillet, then add the broccoli, mushrooms and garlic. Stir, cover and steam for 3 minutes. Add the salt and pepper to the eggs and pour over the broccoli. Sprinkle with the Parmesan cheese and bake, uncovered, for 25 to 30 minutes or until set.

Six servings.

Variation:

Omit the salt to ½ teaspoon and, before baking, add to the eggs ½ pound grated Monterey Jack or Muenster cheese and ⅓ pound salami, cut into thin strips.

❧ ASPARAGUS FRITTATA

4 tablespoons (½ stick) butter
12 fresh asparagus spears, briefly cooked and cut into 1-inch lengths
½ pound fresh mushrooms, sliced
½ pound ham, diced
8 eggs, beaten
Salt
½ teaspoon freshly ground pepper
1 tablespoon Dijon-style mustard

Preheat the oven to 350° F. Melt the butter in a 10-inch skillet. Add the asparagus and mushrooms, stir, cover and cook for about 3 minutes. Add the ham and cook for 2 minutes more. Combine the eggs, salt, pepper and mustard and stir into the pan. Bake in the oven, uncovered, for 25 to 30 minutes or until set.

Six servings.

Variations:

- Sprinkle ½ pound grated Swiss cheese over the eggs before baking.
- Keep 6 asparagus spears whole and arrange them like spokes of a wheel over the eggs before baking.

❧ PASTA FRITTATA

This is one of my favorite ways to use leftover pasta and sauce, especially when there's not quite enough sauce for the leftover pasta. Any kind of pasta and sauce work well here; the variations are infinite. (I often add some red pepper flakes or hot pepper sauce to the eggs if the pasta needs some zip.)

2 green peppers, sliced thin
2 onions, halved vertically, then sliced thin
2 cloves garlic, minced
3 tablespoons olive oil
½ teaspoon freshly ground pepper
4 cups leftover pasta with sauce
¾ cup freshly grated Parmesan cheese
8 eggs, beaten

Preheat the oven to 350° F. In a 10-inch skillet, sauté the peppers, onions and garlic in the olive oil until soft, about 10 minutes, stirring occasionally and seasoning with pepper. Add the pasta and sauce and mix. Beat *½ cup* of the cheese into the eggs and pour into the pan, mixing well with the pasta. Sprinkle the remaining *¼ cup* of cheese on top and bake in the oven, uncovered, for 25 to 30 minutes or until set.

Six servings.

✿ EGGPLANT FRITTATA

1 ½ pounds eggplant, peeled and
  cut into 1-inch dice
3 tablespoons olive or vegetable
  oil
2 onions, halved vertically, then
  sliced thin
2 cloves garlic, minced
8 eggs, beaten
2 teaspoons fresh chopped basil
  or 1 teaspoon dried
Salt
½ teaspoon freshly ground
  pepper
3 tablespoons tomato paste
¾ cup freshly grated Parmesan
  cheese

Preheat the oven to 350° F. Cook the eggplant in boiling salted water for 3 minutes; drain well in a colander. Heat the oil in a 10-inch skillet. Add the onions and garlic, cover and cook for 3 minutes, stirring occasionally. Add the eggplant and cook for 5 minutes more. Beat the eggs with the basil, salt, pepper, tomato paste and ½ cup of the cheese. Pour the egg mixture over the vegetables and stir well. Sprinkle with the remaining ¼ cup cheese and bake in the oven, uncovered, for 25 to 30 minutes or until set.

Six servings.

✿ SAUSAGE AND POTATO FRITTATA

This is good as is, or topped with Homemade Tomato Sauce (p. 87).

3 cups peeled and diced potatoes
½ pound bulk sausage, crumbled
1 onion, diced
8 eggs, beaten
2 to 3 tablespoons chopped fresh
  parsley
1 teaspoon chopped fresh basil or
  ½ teaspoon dried
Salt
¼ teaspoon freshly ground
  pepper
½ cup freshly grated Parmesan
  cheese

Preheat the oven to 350° F. Cook the potatoes in boiling water until done but still firm. Sauté the sausage in its own fat in a 10-inch skillet until cooked through. Remove the sausage to paper towels to drain. Pour off the excess fat from the pan, leaving just enough to film the bottom. Add the onion and cook until translucent, then add the potatoes and cook, covered, over low heat, stirring occasionally, until heated through. Stir in the cooked sausage. Beat the eggs with the parsley, basil, salt, pepper and cheese and stir into the pan, mixing well. Bake in the oven, uncovered, for 25 to 30 minutes or until set.

Six servings.

🌾 NEAPOLITAN FRITTATA

¼ cup olive or vegetable oil
1 pound Italian sausage, sliced
  thin
1 green pepper, chopped
½ cup halved pitted black olives
1 ½ cups coarsely chopped and
  drained tomatoes
1 cup chopped onion
2 cloves garlic, minced
2 teaspoons dried oregano
½ teaspoon salt
½ teaspoon freshly ground
  pepper
½ teaspoon hot red pepper flakes
  (optional)
8 eggs, beaten
½ cup freshly grated Parmesan
  cheese

Preheat the oven to 350° F. Place the oil in a 10-inch skillet, add the sausage and cook, stirring often, for 5 minutes. Add the green pepper, olives, tomatoes, onion, garlic, oregano, salt, pepper and red pepper flakes. Cover, and cook for about 7 minutes, stirring or shaking the pan often until the liquid is mostly evaporated. Remove the pan from the heat, stir in the eggs and top with the cheese. Bake in the oven, uncovered, for 25 to 30 minutes or until set.

Six servings.

BACON–CARROT FRITTATA

Carrots aren't usually found in a frittata, which is exactly why I experimented with this one. Their flavor and color are wonderful here, and because they are shredded, they cook quickly while retaining a bit of crunch. I like to garnish this frittata with cherry tomatoes that have been sautéed for a few minutes in butter.

6 slices bacon

3 tablespoons butter

3 tablespoons minced green onions

3 to 4 carrots, shredded

2 cloves garlic, minced

¼ cup freshly grated Parmesan cheese

2 teaspoons chopped fresh basil or 1 teaspoon dried

2 teaspoons chopped fresh marjoram or 1 teaspoon dried

8 eggs, beaten with 2 tablespoons cold water

Preheat the oven to 350° F. Cook the bacon in a 10-inch skillet over moderate heat until crisp. Drain on paper towels, then crumble. Remove all but 1 tablespoon of the bacon fat from the pan, then add the butter and heat. Add the green onions, carrots and garlic and sauté for 5 to 10 minutes or until softened. Add ½ of the Parmesan cheese, the basil and the marjoram to the beaten eggs and pour over the vegetables. Place the skillet in the oven and bake, uncovered, until the eggs are just set but the top is still slightly liquid, about 25 to 30 minutes. Sprinkle with the bacon and the remaining Parmesan cheese and place under the broiler for about 3 to 5 minutes or until the cheese is melted and lightly browned and the top is firm. Remove, let stand for a few minutes, then cut into wedges and serve.

Six servings.

❧ BASIC PIECRUST (FOR QUICHES AND ALL OTHER PIES)

This foolproof pastry is good for quiches and meat pies, and for dessert pies as well. Double the recipe if you want a 2-crust pie. Add ⅓ cup sugar and 2 tablespoons cocoa for a devilishly delicious chocolate crust.

1 cup flour
¼ teaspoon salt
6 tablespoons butter or 3
*   tablespoons butter and 3*
*   tablespoons shortening*
1 egg yolk
1 to 2 tablespoons ice water

Preheat the oven to 400° F. Combine all the ingredients in a medium mixing bowl. With your fingers, a pastry blender or 2 knives, work the mixture together until fine crumbs are formed. Add the ice water, a little at a time, until the dough is moist enough to form a ball. Wrap the dough in waxed paper and chill for about 1 hour. Pat the chilled dough into a 9-inch pie plate or roll on a pastry cloth, forming a 13-inch circle, then fit into the pie plate. Trim and flute the edge. Prick the bottom of the crust all over with a fork. Bake in the oven until golden brown, 10 to 15 minutes, or fill and bake according to a pie recipe.

One 9-inch pie shell.

❧ TOMATO–ONION QUICHE

Basic Piecrust pastry (see above)
1 egg, separated
2 tablespoons butter
2 medium onions, sliced thin
2 medium ripe tomatoes, peeled,
*   seeded, diced and well drained*
½ teaspoon sugar
¼ teaspoon salt
⅛ teaspoon freshly ground
*   pepper*
1 cup grated sharp Cheddar
*   cheese*
2 whole eggs
1¼ cups milk, scalded

Preheat the oven to 375° F. Fit the pastry into a 9-inch quiche dish or pie pan. Crimp the dough over edge of the dish and trim. Brush gently with the egg white. Melt the butter in an 8½-inch skillet over low heat. Add the onions and cook until limp but not browned. Spread the onions and butter over the bottom of the pastry. Spread the tomatoes over the onions. Blend the sugar, salt and pepper and sprinkle over the tomatoes, then sprinkle evenly with the cheese. In a small mixing bowl, beat the egg yolk with the whole eggs. Beating constantly, add the hot milk gradually. Pour the egg mixture into the filled pastry shell and bake in the oven for 35 to 40 minutes or until the custard is set.

Six servings.

❧ COUNTRY QUICHE

Sausage and apples make this a festive brunch or luncheon dish.

Double recipe of Basic Piecrust
  pastry (p. 105)
1 egg, separated
1 ¼ pounds bulk pork sausage,
  cooked and crumbled
2 or 3 apples, peeled and sliced
  thin
¾ cup coarsely chopped pecans or
  walnuts
1 ½ cups shredded mild Cheddar
  cheese
3 whole eggs
½ teaspoon salt
2 cups milk, scalded

Preheat the oven to 425° F. Fit the pastry into a 12-inch quiche dish. Crimp the dough over the edge of the dish and trim. Brush with the egg white. Partially bake the crust for 7 to 10 minutes. Remove from the oven and reduce the heat to 375° F. Spread the sausage evenly over the crust. Arrange the apple slices in a single layer over the sausage. Sprinkle with the pecans, then add the cheese. In a medium mixing bowl, beat the egg yolk with the whole eggs and the salt. Beating constantly, add the hot milk gradually. Pour the egg mixture into the filled shell. Bake in the oven for 45 to 50 minutes or until the custard is set and the apples are crisp-tender.

Eight to ten servings.

❧ ZUCCHINI–MUSHROOM QUICHE

Basic Piecrust pastry (p. 105)
2 tablespoons butter
2 tablespoons vegetable or corn oil
3 green onions, minced
4 small zucchini, sliced into very
  thin strips
½ cup sliced fresh mushrooms
3 eggs
1 cup light cream or
  half-and-half
½ teaspoon salt
¼ teaspoon freshly ground
  pepper
¾ cup grated sharp Cheddar
  cheese

Preheat the oven to 425° F. Fit the pastry into a 9-inch quiche dish or pie pan. Crimp the dough over the edge of the dish and trim. Partially bake the crust for about 7 to 10 minutes. Remove from the oven and reduce the heat to 375° F. Melt the butter and oil in a 10-inch skillet. Add the green onions, zucchini and mushrooms and sauté for 5 to 10 minutes; spoon into the partially baked shell. Mix together the eggs, cream, salt and pepper and pour over the vegetables in the pie shell. Top with the grated cheese. Bake in the oven for 25 minutes or until set.

Six servings.

❧ JOE'S SPECIAL

An old-time San Francisco favorite, great for late-night snacks.

3 tablespoons olive oil
1 pound lean *ground beef*
1 clove garlic, minced
1 onion, chopped
½ pound fresh mushrooms, sliced
2 packages (10 ounces each) frozen chopped spinach
1 teaspoon chopped fresh basil or *½ teaspoon dried*
1 teaspoon chopped fresh marjoram or oregano or *½ teaspoon dried*
1 teaspoon salt
½ teaspoon freshly ground pepper
6 eggs, beaten

Heat the oil in a 10-inch skillet and brown the meat in it, breaking it up with a fork. Add the garlic, onion and mushrooms and cook for about 5 minutes, stirring. Cook the spinach briefly and drain well. And the spinach, basil, marjoram or oregano, salt and pepper to the meat mixture and cook for 2 minutes more. Stir in the eggs and cook, stirring, until set.

Four servings.

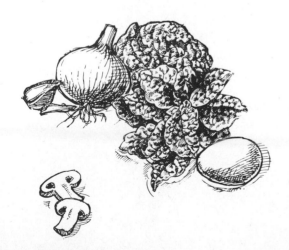

❧ HANGTOWN FRY

How elegant this is as an aftertheater midnight supper—do try it with sparkling white wine or champagne.

¼ pound bacon, diced
12 fresh oysters, shucked, drained
*   and halved*
2 eggs, beaten
25 soda crackers, crushed
8 eggs
⅓ cup heavy cream
¼ cup chopped fresh parsley
¼ cup chopped chives or green
*   onion tops*
½ teaspoon salt
½ teaspoon freshly ground
*   pepper*
⅓ cup freshly grated Parmesan
*   cheese*

Fry the bacon until crisp; drain on paper towels. Remove all but 6 tablespoons of bacon fat from the pan. Dip the oysters into the beaten egg and then into the cracker crumbs. Heat the bacon fat over moderate heat and fry the oysters in it until golden. Beat the eggs with the cream, parsley, chives or green onion tops, salt and pepper. Pour the egg mixture over the oysters, add the bacon and reduce the heat to low. Scramble the eggs gently, lifting the cooked egg with a fork so that the uncooked egg runs underneath. When the eggs are just set but still moist, sprinkle with the cheese and run under the broiler for a few seconds.

Four servings.

❧ CHEESE SOUFFLÉ

This is an easy, economical family dish, nice with Homemade Tomato Sauce
(p. 87). Try it without the ham as a first course the next time you have guests.

Freshly grated Parmesan cheese
3 tablespoons butter
3 tablespoons flour
¾ cup milk
¼ teaspoon dry mustard
½ teaspoon salt
½ teaspoon freshly ground
 pepper
1 cup shredded provolone, Swiss
 or Cheddar cheese
½ cup finely minced ham
 (optional)
3 eggs, separated

Preheat the oven to 375° F. Butter a 1½-quart soufflé
dish or straight-sided casserole; sprinkle the buttered
sides and bottom with grated Parmesan cheese. In a
1-quart saucepan, melt the 3 tablespoons butter and
stir in the flour; cook, stirring constantly, for 3 to 4
minutes. Add the milk, mustard, salt and pepper and
continue to cook, stirring, to the boiling point. Allow
to boil for 1 minute, stir in the cheese (and ham, if
desired) and set aside. Put the egg yolks into a small
mixing bowl and stir in a little of the cheese sauce to
warm the yolks. Gradually fold the yolks into the
cheese mixture in the saucepan. Beat the egg whites in
another mixing bowl until stiff. Carefully fold a gener-
ous dollop of beaten egg white into the egg yolk-
cheese mixture, then fold everything together carefully and gently (it is not necessary to mix completely).
Pour the mixture into the prepared soufflé dish. Bake
for 15 to 20 minutes for a soft soufflé or 20 to 25
minutes for a firmer one.

Four to six servings.

❧ DEEP-SOUTH SPOON BREAD

I wish I had known about spoon bread, a sort of dense soufflé, when I was a child. After all, we did live slightly south—of Albany, New York, that is. Now that I make it, I find it's delicious served with lots of butter or with a sauce, accompanying chicken or game.

3 cups milk
1 ½ teaspoons salt
1 cup cornmeal
2 tablespoons butter
3 eggs, separated
1 tablespoon baking powder

Preheat the oven to 375° F. In a 2-quart saucepan, combine the milk and salt. Bring to a boil, stirring frequently, then reduce to a simmer. Slowly add the cornmeal, stirring constantly, until it thickens. Add the butter, stirring until it is completely absorbed. Remove from the heat. Beat the egg yolks and baking powder together and slowly beat this into the hot mixture; let cool slightly. Beat the egg whites until stiff and fold into the cooling cornmeal mixture. Pour the entire mixture into a 1½-quart buttered baking dish and bake in the oven for about 40 minutes or until puffed and browned. Serve hot.

Six servings.

Variations:

- Add 4 slices crumbled fried bacon to the batter.
- Add 1 to 2 finely chopped and seeded green chilies to the batter and serve with Cornelius's Chili (p. 43).

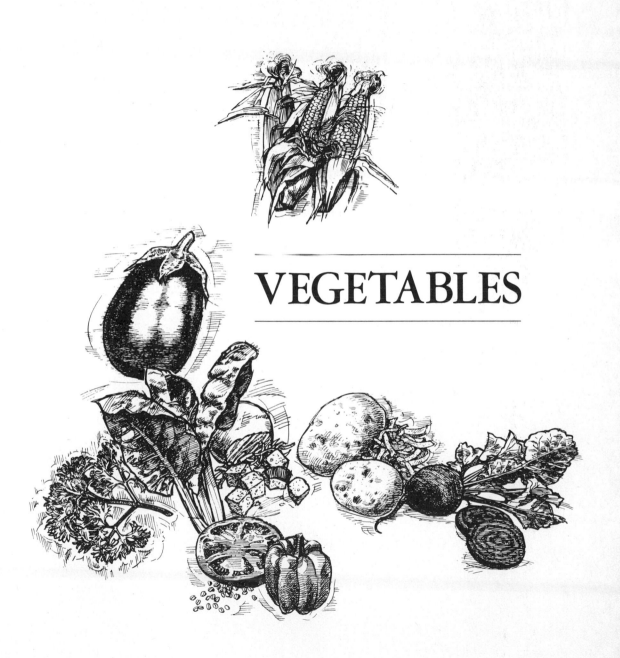

VEGETABLES

❧ CRUNCHY ASPARAGUS

The secret to this or any other "stir-fry" is to have all the ingredients premeasured and set out on a tray near the stove. (For another great way to serve asparagus, see Asparagus Frittata, p. 101.)

2 tablespoons vegetable or corn oil
1 pound fresh asparagus, cut
   into 2-inch lengths
2 teaspoons soy sauce
1 teaspoon grated fresh ginger or
   ½ teaspoon powdered
½ cup sliced water chestnuts
Freshly ground pepper

Heat the oil in an 8½-inch skillet over moderate heat. Sauté the asparagus in the oil for 5 minutes. Add the remaining ingredients and cook for 3 minutes, stirring. Cover and cook for about 5 minutes more, stirring once or twice, until the asparagus is just tender but still crunchy.

Four to six servings.

❧ ASPARAGUS BAKED IN FOIL

You can also make this in a covered shallow casserole that goes straight from the oven to the table.

1 ½ pounds fresh asparagus
3 tablespoons butter
3 tablespoons fresh lemon juice
2 tablespoons finely chopped green
   onions
Salt
Freshly ground pepper

Preheat the oven to 425° F. Wash the asparagus, snapping off the tough ends of the stems. Place on a large sheet of foil. Melt the butter in a small saucepan, add the lemon juice and green onions and season with salt and pepper. Pour this mixture over the asparagus and wrap, folding the foil over the asparagus and crimping the edges together. Bake for 30 to 45 minutes or until tender.

Four servings.

❧ GREEN BEANS VINAIGRETTE

2 pounds fresh green beans
Lemon Vinaigrette Dressing (p.
* 133)*

Wash the beans and trim them if necessary. Drop them into a 6-quart pot of rapidly boiling, salted water. Cook quickly, uncovered, until crisp-tender. Drain the beans in a colander under running cold water, transfer to a serving bowl and toss with the dressing. Let cool to room temperature before serving.

Six to eight servings.

Variation:

To serve these as a cocktail nibble, omit the dressing; just drain, sprinkle with coarse salt and pass at once, while they're still hot. Your guests will gobble them up in seconds.

❧ SPICY BEETS

To cook fresh beets, cut off the tops except for about an inch of stem, put them into rapidly boiling water and cook until fork-tender. This can take anywhere from 30 minutes to 1 hour, depending on the age and size of the beets. When done, hold them under cold water and slip off the skins.

1 tablespoon sugar or honey
1 tablespoon prepared
* horseradish*
⅛ teaspoon celery seed
¼ teaspoon salt (or to taste)
Dash of paprika
1 tablespoon vinegar
⅓ cup sour cream
3 cups diced cooked beets

Mix all the ingredients except the beets over low heat in a 2-quart saucepan. Stir in the beets, cover and simmer for about 10 minutes, stirring from time to time. Do not boil.

Six servings.

❧ BAKED BROCCOLI AND CAULIFLOWER

A green-and-white delight. Use leftover broccoli in Broccoli Frittata (p. 100), another splendid broccoli dish.

1 tablespoon butter
2 tablespoons flour
½ cup milk
½ teaspoon salt
Dash of freshly ground pepper
⅓ cup shredded Cheddar cheese
½ cup sour cream
¼ cup vegetable or corn oil
½ pound cauliflower, cut into
  bite-sized pieces (about 2 cups)
½ pound broccoli, cut into
  bite-sized pieces (about 2 cups)
1 cup sliced fresh mushrooms
¼ cup sliced green onions

Preheat the oven to 350° F. Melt the butter in a small saucepan, add flour and stir over moderate heat for 3 to 4 minutes. Add the milk, stirring constantly, until the sauce reaches the boiling point and thickens. Reduce the heat to low and cook for 2 minutes, adding the salt, pepper and cheese. Cook until the cheese melts. Remove from the heat, add the sour cream, and stir until blended; set aside. Heat the oil in a 10-inch skillet over moderate heat. Add the cauliflower and broccoli, tossing continuously to coat with the oil and prevent burning; cook for 2 minutes. Add the mushrooms and green onions and continue tossing for another minute or so; remove from the heat. In a buttered 1½-quart casserole, put a layer of the sauce, add half the vegetables, spread with more sauce, add the remaining vegetables, and cover with the remaining sauce. Bake, covered, for 20 minutes.

Four to five servings.

Variation:

If you like your broccoli crunchy (as I do), reserve some flowerets and add them, uncooked, to the casserole before baking.

❧ STEAMED CABBAGE

Cabbage is often considered the "poor relation" of the vegetable family, mainly because it is usually overcooked and soggy. Try it this way—with a definite crunch—and you'll welcome it back into your home.

½ head cabbage (about 1
  pound)
3 tablespoons butter
½ cup cream (optional)

Remove center core of the cabbage and discard. Shred the cabbage. Melt the butter in a 10-inch skillet. Dump the cabbage on top of the butter, cover and steam for 3 to 5 minutes, tasting and stirring often to be sure that the cabbage remains slightly crunchy. Stir in the cream, if you wish, during the last 2 minutes of cooking.

Four to six servings.

Variation:

Before serving, toss the cabbage with ½ teaspoon caraway seed or toasted sesame seeds.

❧ CITRUS CARROTS

The flavors of orange and carrot complement each other so well. Just think of how many entrées would benefit from this culinary synergy: chicken, duck, pork, even fish.

2 tablespoons butter
1 pound carrots, sliced thin
¼ teaspoon grated orange peel
  (orange part only)
2 tablespoons orange juice
Pinch of dried marjoram

Place all the ingredients in an 8½-inch skillet. Cook over low heat until the carrots are well glazed and just tender, about 15 to 20 minutes, shaking occasionally to prevent sticking.

Four servings.

❧ CARROT PANCAKES

I like to serve these topped with sour cream or yogurt as a side dish with meat or chicken.

2 eggs, beaten
2 teaspoons sour cream
2 teaspoons molasses
⅓ cup flour
1 ½ cups grated carrots
1 teaspoon grated orange peel
  (orange part only)
Salt
Freshly ground pepper
Butter (for frying)

Preheat the oven to 200° F. Combine all the ingredients except the butter and mix well with a whisk or electric beater. Heat the butter in an 8½-inch skillet. Ladle enough batter onto the skillet to make silver-dollar-sized pancakes (or larger if you prefer). When the pancakes are nicely browned on one side, flip them over and brown the other side. Keep them warm in the oven until all the batter is used.

Four to six servings.

❧ MOROCCAN CARROTS

I got this recipe from an English friend. It was always a great hit at her dinner table, now at mine and soon, I hope, at yours. It's ideal for buffets, for it tastes best at room temperature. (For yet another delicious carrot recipe, see Bacon–Carrot Frittata, p. 104.)

2 pounds carrots
½ cup water
6 tablespoons olive oil
2 cloves garlic, minced
1 to 2 tablespoons vinegar
Salt
Freshly ground pepper
½ teaspoon powdered cumin
¼ teaspoon powdered cardamom
1 to 2 tablespoons finely chopped
  fresh parsley
⅓ cup sunflower seeds, roasted

Quarter the carrots lengthwise and cut them into 2-inch sticks. Place them in a 10-inch skillet. Add the water, oil and garlic and simmer until the carrots can be pierced with a fork but are still underdone and very firm; drain and transfer to a serving bowl. Add the vinegar and spices, using more than the specified amounts if desired, until the carrots are flavored to taste. Add the parsley and sunflower seeds. Serve at room temperature.

Six servings.

❧ CELERY AND TOMATOES

Easy to prepare, always a great success.

3 cups thinly sliced celery
1 can (16 ounces) stewed
   tomatoes with liquid
Salt
Freshly ground pepper
2 teaspoons chopped fresh basil
   or 1 teaspoon dried
½ to 1 cup bread crumbs

Preheat the oven to 350° F. Cook the celery in a minimal amount of water until tender but still slightly crisp. Stir in the tomatoes, salt, pepper and basil. Place the vegetables in a small casserole and top with the crumbs. Bake for 15 to 20 minutes or until the top is bubbly.

Four to six servings.

❧ CORN PANCAKES

These are nifty served with applesauce or sour cream, great with fried chicken, pork or sausage.

2 eggs, beaten
2 tablespoons light cream or sour
   cream
2 tablespoons butter, melted
1 ½ cups frozen corn, thawed, or
   cooked corn cut from the cob
2 teaspoons molasses
¼ cup flour
Salt
Freshly ground pepper
More butter (for frying)

Preheat the oven to 200° F. Combine all the ingredients, except the butter for frying, blending well. Heat some butter in an 8½-inch skillet. Ladle the batter into the skillet to make silver-dollar-sized pancakes (or larger if you prefer). When the pancakes are nicely browned on one side flip them over and brown the other side. Keep them warm in the oven until all the batter is used.

Four to six servings.

❦ YORKSHIRE CORN PUDDING

I like to serve this with roast pork. They go well together, and the meat provides nice, fatty pan drippings for flavoring and cooking the pudding.

¼ cup pan drippings from a roast (or use butter)
1 cup flour
1 teaspoon salt
2 eggs
1 cup milk
1 ½ cups cooked fresh corn or 1 package (10 ounces) frozen corn, thawed

Preheat the oven to 400° F. Place the drippings or butter in a flat 9-by-13-by-2-inch baking dish. Place the dish in the oven while mixing the remaining ingredients (except the corn), using a whisk or blender. Stir in the corn. Pour the mixture into the hot baking dish, tilting the dish to spread the batter evenly. Bake for 25 minutes or until browned and crisp. Serve at once.

Four to six servings.

❦ FRIED MUSHROOMS

Try these as an appetizer or as a side dish. They're great either way.

1 pound fresh firm mushrooms
¾ cup cracker meal or fine cracker crumbs
1 egg, beaten with 2 tablespoons water
1 quart vegetable oil
Salt
Freshly ground pepper

Dip the mushrooms into the cracker crumbs, then into the beaten egg and water and again into the cracker crumbs. Let stand, uncovered, while the oil is heating. Heat the oil in a 4-quart saucepan to 375° F. Cook ¼ of the mushrooms at a time, frying them until well browned, then draining on paper towels. Sprinkle with salt and pepper before serving.

Four servings.

◦✼◦ BAKED BOURBON ONIONS WITH MORNAY SAUCE

These are just fine without the bourbon, too!

6 Spanish onions or 8 to 10
   yellow onions
2 tablespoons butter
Freshly ground pepper
Bourbon
¼ cup water

Preheat the oven to 350° F. Peel and trim the onions but leave them whole. Cut a small hole out of the blossom end of each onion. Place the onions, hole side *up*, in a 12-by-8-inch baking dish. Put a dab of butter into each hole, sprinkle with pepper and a few drops of bourbon. Pour the water into the bottom of the dish, cover with foil and bake for 1½ hours. Serve with Mornay Sauce (p. 130).

Six servings.

Variation:

Sprinkle the finished dish with crumbled crisp pieces of bacon.

◦✼◦ SHREDDED POTATOES WITH FENNEL

Serve these plain or with Homemade Tomato Sauce (p. 87).

3 tablespoons butter
4 large potatoes, peeled and
   shredded
1 medium onion, chopped fine
1 teaspoon fennel seed, crushed
Salt
Freshly ground pepper

Melt the butter in a 10-inch skillet. Mix the potatoes, onion and seasonings and add to the skillet. Press into a flat cake with a spatula. Cook over low heat for 30 minutes or more or until the potatoes are soft and heavily crusted on their underside. To serve, slice into 4 individual portions.

Four servings.

CORN PANCAKES

CRUNCHY ASPARAGUS *and* MOROCCAN CARROTS

ITALIAN TOMATO SALAD

(L to R)
DAY-AFTER-THANKSGIVING SQUASH, ZUCCHINI PANCAKES,

POTATO PANCAKES *and* SUMMER SQUASH SKILLET

SPINACH-ONION-ORANGE SALAD

◦❧◦ POTATOES ANNA

This classic is one of my all-time favorites. The potatoes retain the shape of
the dish in which they are cooked and form an attractive cake of brown,
overlapped slices.

4 baking potatoes
2 cups ice water
1 tablespoon fresh lemon juice
2 or more tablespoons butter
Paprika
Salt
Freshly ground pepper
Parsley sprigs
Chopped fresh chives

Preheat the oven to 400° F. Butter a 9-inch pie plate
very generously. Peel the potatoes and slice them into
¼-inch-thick rounds. As you slice them, put them in
ice water and lemon juice to prevent discoloration.
Drain and dry the potatoes and arrange them in a layer
in the bottom of the pie plate in a spiral, beginning in
the center and continuing outward, with the potato
slices overlapping. Dot generously with butter and
sprinkle with paprika, salt and pepper. Repeat, making
2 or 3 layers in all. Dot the top with butter and sprinkle again with paprika, salt and pepper. Immediately
cover with a lid or foil and bake for about 30 minutes.
Remove the cover and continue baking until the
potatoes are tender and browned on top, about 10 to
15 minutes more. Invert the potatoes onto a broilerproof platter and run them under the broiler for a few
minutes until browned. Serve at once, garnished with
parsley and chives.

Four servings.

Variation:

Add layers of very thinly sliced onion between each
potato layer.

✺ MASHED POTATOES WITH GREEN ONIONS

6 medium potatoes, peeled and
  quartered
1 bay leaf
4 green onions or shallots,
  minced
4 tablespoons (½ stick) butter
About ⅓ cup heavy cream
Salt
Freshly ground pepper
Dash of nutmeg

Cover the potatoes and bay leaf with cold water. Bring to a boil and cook until the potatoes are tender. Drain well, then shake the pan with the potatoes in it over the hot burner to dry them. Remove the bay leaf. While the potatoes are boiling, sauté the green onions or shallots in the butter until tender. Add them to the cooked, drained potatoes and mash all together with a potato masher or electric beater, adding just enough cream for a smooth consistency and flavoring to taste with salt, pepper and nutmeg.

Four servings.

✺ DILLED NEW POTATOES

These are lovely with fish. Use coarse salt in this recipe if you have it.

1 ½ pounds new potatoes
  (uniform in size)
Butter
Salt
1 ½ tablespoons chopped fresh
  dill or 1 tablespoon dried

Wash the potatoes but do not peel them. Cook them in boiling, salted water until just tender. Drain well, then toss with plenty of butter, salt and dill. Serve at once.

Four servings.

Variations:

Instead of dill, toss with finely chopped pistachio nuts or a mixture of chopped watercress and parsley.

❧ POMMES DAUPHINOISES

If any of these potatoes are left over, try serving them cold the next day, splashed with a little cider vinegar.

2 cups heavy cream
4 cloves garlic, minced
6 medium potatoes

Preheat the oven to 350° F. Place the heavy cream and garlic in a 2½-quart saucepan and bring to a slow simmer. Peel the potatoes and slice them directly into the cream. Raise the heat to moderate and stir constantly; as the slices heat, they will release potato starch, which will thicken the cream. When the cream starts to thicken (usually just as it starts to boil), pour the cream, garlic and potatoes into a buttered shallow 2½-quart casserole. Bake for 25 to 30 minutes.

Four to six servings.

❧ POTATO PANCAKES

There's a reason why I have a special affinity for these: My 110-pound mother once ate twenty-seven at one sitting. Three or four hours later, I came into the world! I've been grating potatoes ever since.

Potato pancakes are traditionally served with applesauce, and sometimes with sour cream and chives. I have been known to serve them with both, because I can't decide which I like better. These are a little unusual because of the cheese—unusually delicious, that is.

4 medium potatoes
2 tablespoons flour
2 tablespoons mayonnaise
3 tablespoons grated onion
2 eggs
¼ cup light cream
½ cup grated sharp Cheddar cheese
Salt
Freshly ground pepper
Butter (for frying)

Preheat the oven to 200° F. Peel the potatoes and grate them in a food processor or onto a paper towel or clean tea towel; squeeze to remove some of the moisture. Combine them with the remaining ingredients except the butter. Heat some butter in a 10-inch skillet. Ladle the batter into the skillet to make silver-dollar-sized pancakes (or larger if you prefer). When the pancakes are nicely browned on one side, flip them over and brown the other side. Keep them warm in the oven until all the batter is used.

About two dozen small pancakes.

❧ PECAN SWEET POTATOES

A nice, festive touch for the Thanksgiving turkey.

6 medium sweet potatoes
4 tablespoons (½ stick) butter
1 cup firmly packed light brown
  sugar
¼ cup orange juice
1 tablespoon grated orange peel
  (orange part only)
½ teaspoon salt (or to taste)
¾ cup coarsely chopped pecans

Preheat the oven to 400° F. Bake the potatoes in the oven for 50 to 60 minutes or until tender. Remove the potatoes from the oven and reduce the heat to 350° F. Let the potatoes cool until they can be handled, then remove the skins and cut the potatoes in half lengthwise. Melt the butter in a roasting pan and stir in the sugar, orange juice, orange peel and salt. Cook, stirring, over low heat for 10 minutes. Add the potatoes, turning each piece in the butter mixture to coat. Bake for 30 minutes, basting and turning the potatoes twice. Sprinkle with pecans and serve.

Six servings.

❧ OUT-OF-THE-RUT RUTABAGA

I love turnips of all kinds, especially the large yellow turnip known as rutabaga. It has a sweetness that belies its coarse appearance. Serve it with pot roast or other gravied meats.

2 ½ pounds rutabaga, peeled
  and cut into ½-inch cubes
2 cups beef or vegetable broth
1 tablespoon chopped fresh dill
  or 1 teaspoon dried
Salt
Freshly ground pepper
Butter

In a 2½-quart saucepan, cook the rutabaga in the broth over low heat until tender, about 45 to 60 minutes, depending on the desired firmness. Drain, season with dill, salt and pepper and serve with butter, or gravy, if you have some, from the main course.

Four servings.

SAUTÉED SPINACH WITH PINE NUTS

1 pound fresh spinach
2 tablespoons olive oil
½ cup chopped green onions
About 2 tablespoons pine nuts or chopped walnuts
Dash of nutmeg
½ lemon

Wash the spinach and trim away the coarse stems. Bring a 5-quart pot of water to a boil, add the spinach and cook for 30 seconds. Drain well and, when cool, squeeze dry and chop. Heat the olive oil in a 10-inch skillet. Sauté the green onions until transparent, then add the nuts and cook briefly until golden. Add the spinach and stir for about 1 minute or until heated through. Sprinkle with the nutmeg, add a squeeze of lemon and serve.

Three to four servings.

SPINACH CREPES

Serve with Mornay Sauce (p. 130) for an elegant touch.

½ pound chopped fresh spinach or 1 package (10 ounces) chopped, frozen
1 ½ cups ricotta cheese
¼ cup freshly grated Romano cheese
1 egg, beaten
2 tablespoons chopped fresh parsley
Freshly ground pepper
8 crepes (p. 64)
Butter

Preheat the oven to 350° F. Cook the spinach; drain and squeeze dry. Combine with the ricotta cheese, Romano cheese, egg and parsley; season with pepper and mix well. Fill the crepes and place them, seam side *down,* in a buttered 13-by-9-inch baking dish. Dot with butter or top with Mornay Sauce. Bake until bubbly, about 25 minutes.

Four to six servings.

❧ SPINACH PANCAKES

Spinach Pancakes are a perfect foil for plain broiled fish, or top them with Hollandaise Sauce (p. 130) for a wonderful vegetarian lunch.

1 package (10 ounces) frozen
  chopped spinach
2 eggs, beaten
2 tablespoons mayonnaise
1 teaspoon chopped fresh
  tarragon or ½ teaspoon dried
¼ cup flour
¼ cup freshly grated Parmesan
  cheese
¼ cup chopped fresh mushrooms
  (optional)
Freshly ground pepper
Butter (for frying)

Preheat the oven to 200° F. Defrost the spinach and squeeze it dry. Combine all the ingredients except the butter and mix well. Melt some butter in an 8½-inch skillet. Ladle the batter into the skillet to make silver-dollar-sized pancakes (or larger if you prefer). When the pancakes are nicely browned on one side, flip them over and brown the other side. Keep them warm in the oven until all the batter is used.

Four servings.

❧ NEW ENGLAND ACORN SQUASH

A dish to perk up any winter meal.

1 small acorn squash (8 to 12
  ounces)
2 tablespoons maple syrup
1 tablespoon butter, softened
1 tablespoon dry sherry
⅛ teaspoon nutmeg

Preheat the oven to 375° F. Cut the squash in half; remove the seeds and fibers. Place the halves, cut side up, in a casserole. Divide the remaining ingredients between the squash halves, filling the cavities. Pour ½ cup water around the squash. Bake for 50 minutes or until fork-tender, basting several times with the syrup mixture. Drain and serve.

Two servings.

DAY-AFTER-THANKSGIVING SQUASH

Here's a nifty way to use Thanksgiving leftovers. It seems so obvious, I wonder why it's not done more often. The squash should be served with sliced leftover turkey, of course.

2 whole acorn squash
¼ cup raw cranberries or *½ cup whole cranberry sauce*
2 cups leftover turkey stuffing
½ cup chopped apple (unpeeled)
½ cup raisins
Salt
Freshly ground pepper
Butter
½ cup apple juice

Preheat the oven to 350° F. Cut the squash in half; remove the seeds and fibers. Place the halves, cut side *down,* in a lightly buttered 9-by-13-inch baking dish. Bake until tender, about 40 minutes. While the squash halves are cooking, make the stuffing: If you are using raw cranberries, you can either leave them whole or chop them coarsely. In a mixing bowl, combine the cranberries or cranberry sauce, the turkey stuffing, chopped apple, raisins, salt and pepper. When the squash are done, turn them cut side *up,* slicing off a piece of the curved underside if necessary to make them sit flat. (Don't make a hole in the shell, though.) Prick the inside of the squash with a fork, dot each cavity with some butter, and spoon *2 tablespoons* of the apple juice into each cavity. Prick again with a fork to allow the juice to soak into the squash. Divide the stuffing mixture among the 4 squash cavities, piling it in firmly. Bake for 15 minutes.

Four servings.

❧ BROILED TOMATOES WITH FRESH HERBS

Do not overcook the tomatoes. They should remain firm and hold their shape.

2 firm, ripe tomatoes
Freshly ground pepper
*1 to 2 teaspoons chopped fresh
    basil*
*1 to 2 teaspoons chopped fresh
    parsley*
Bread crumbs
Freshly grated Parmesan cheese
Butter

Preheat the broiler. Slice the tomatoes in half and arrange them, cut side *up,* in a shallow baking pan or casserole. (Slice off just enough of the bottoms of the tomatoes so that they sit flat.) Sprinkle each half with pepper, basil, parsley and enough bread crumbs and cheese to cover the tops. Dot with butter and place them under the broiler until the crumbs are browned.

Four servings.

❧ ZUCCHINI PANCAKES

These pancakes are one of my favorite side dishes with just about anything. I also like to serve them as a luncheon dish, topped with sour cream and chives or with Homemade Tomato Sauce (p. 87).

½ pound zucchini (unpeeled)
2 eggs, beaten
2 tablespoons mayonnaise
*2 tablespoons finely chopped
    onion*
*¼ cup freshly grated Parmesan
    cheese*
¼ cup flour
*½ teaspoon chopped fresh
    oregano* or *¼ teaspoon dried*
Salt
Pepper
Butter (for frying)

Preheat the oven to 200° F. Grate the zucchini in a food processor or onto paper towels or a clean tea towel and squeeze to remove some of the moisture. Combine all the ingredients except the butter and mix well. Melt some butter in an 8½-inch skillet. Ladle the batter into the skillet to make silver-dollar-sized pancakes (or larger if you prefer). When the pancakes are nicely browned on one side, flip them over and brown the other side. Keep them warm in the oven until all the batter is used.

Four to six servings.

❧ BREADED ZUCCHINI CIRCLES

I often serve these as an appetizer before dinner.

1 ½ pounds zucchini
½ cup mayonnaise
1 egg, slightly beaten
1 cup bread crumbs
½ teaspoon freshly ground
  pepper
½ cup freshly grated Parmesan
  cheese

Preheat the oven to 400° F. Slice the zucchini into ¼-inch-thick circles or cut it into strips. Mix the mayonnaise and egg together, and dip each zucchini slice into the mixture. Mix the bread crumbs with the pepper and Parmesan cheese and spread this mixture out on a flat plate. Press each zucchini slice into the bread-crumb mixture, coating all sides. Arrange the coated slices on a lightly greased cookie sheet and bake for about 25 to 30 minutes or until the slices are golden brown, turning once. The zucchini should be tender on the inside but crisp on the outside.

Three to four servings.

❧ SUMMER SQUASH SKILLET

A colorful tribute to the best of summer's plenty.

4 tablespoons (½ stick) butter
4 small zucchini, cut into ¼-
  inch-thick rounds
3 small yellow crookneck squash,
  cut into ¼-inch-thick rounds
1 medium onion, sliced thin
¼ cup water
2 teaspoons chopped fresh
  tarragon or 1 teaspoon dried
Salt
Freshly ground pepper
2 small tomatoes, quartered

Melt the butter in a 3-quart saucepan. Add the zucchini, yellow squash, onion and water. Cover, and cook over moderate heat for 10 minutes. Sprinkle with the tarragon and add salt and pepper to taste. Add the tomatoes and cook, uncovered, for 3 minutes longer. Serve with the pan juices, either hot or at room temperature.

Four to six servings.

✤ MORNAY SAUCE (FOR JUST ABOUT ANY VEGETABLE)

4 tablespoons (½ stick) butter
¼ cup flour
½ teaspoon salt (or to taste)
¼ teaspoon freshly ground
  pepper
1 cup milk
1 cup chicken broth
½ onion
1 cup grated Swiss cheese
½ teaspoon Worcestershire sauce

Melt the butter in a 1-quart saucepan. Add the flour, salt and pepper and cook, stirring, about 3 to 4 minutes, until smooth and bubbling. Gradually add the milk and chicken broth. Add the onion in 1 piece. Cook over low heat, stirring constantly, until the sauce reaches the boiling point and thickens. Remove from the heat; discard the onion. Add the cheese and Worcestershire sauce, stirring until the cheese has melted.

About two cups.

✤ HOLLANDAISE SAUCE

Delicious but loaded with calories. The trick to Hollandaise Sauce is to use low heat and stir *constantly.* It's guaranteed to add elegance to cooked eggs, fish or vegetables, in addition to being luscious with Spinach Pancakes (p. 126).

2 egg yolks
3 tablespoons fresh lemon juice
¼ pound (1 stick) butter, chilled
⅛ teaspoon salt (or to taste)
Freshly ground pepper

Using a wooden spoon, blend the egg yolks and lemon juice in the top of a double boiler over hot, *not boiling,* water. Add *4 tablespoons* of the chilled butter. Cook, stirring vigorously, until the butter is melted. Add the remaining *4 tablespoons* chilled butter and continue cooking and stirring until the sauce is thickened. Season with salt and pepper and serve either hot or lukewarm.

One cup.

SALADS

❦ GREEN SALAD WITH CHOICE OF TWO VINAIGRETTE DRESSINGS

Choose the freshest, crispest greens, allowing a good handful per person: bibb or Boston lettuce, watercress or arugula leaves, romaine or chicory. (Avoid iceberg lettuce, which has so little taste.) Wash in cold water and shake or spin dry. Wrap in terry toweling and refrigerate if you are not going to use it immediately. Add chopped fresh parsley and any other fresh herbs you may have on hand. Toss in vinaigrette dressing before serving.

BASIC VINAIGRETTE DRESSING:

¼ cup wine vinegar
¾ cup olive oil
¼ teaspoon dry mustard
1 large clove garlic, minced
Salt
Freshly ground pepper

Combine all the ingredients in a jar, cover and shake well before using.

One cup.

LEMON VINAIGRETTE DRESSING:

¼ cup fresh lemon juice
Yellow skin of 1 lemon, chopped fine
Salt
Freshly ground pepper
⅛ teaspoon hot red pepper flakes or hot pepper sauce
2 cloves garlic, minced
⅔ cup oil

Combine all ingredients in a jar, cover and shake well before using.

About one cup.

ITALIAN TOMATO SALAD

I often add thin strips of mozzarella cheese to this salad. Sometimes I also add black olives and anchovies, and presto—antipasto! For a beautiful buffet dish, try alternating cheese and tomato slices in a pinwheel pattern before pouring on the dressing.

4 ripe beefsteak tomatoes
2 to 3 cloves garlic, slivered or
* minced*
1 to 2 tablespoons chopped fresh
* basil or 2 teaspoons dried*
2 tablespoons chopped fresh
* parsley*
Salt
Freshly ground pepper
1 tablespoon olive oil
4 tablespoons cider vinegar
Sprinkle of hot red pepper flakes

Slice the tomatoes into a 1-quart glass bowl. Combine the remaining ingredients, pour this over tomatoes, toss and let stand for 1 hour or more. Serve at room temperature.

Four to six servings.

DILLED CUCUMBER SALAD

An all-season standby, this keeps for days in the refrigerator. To serve, remove the cucumbers from the marinade with a slotted spoon and arrange them on curly-leaf lettuce. Ring the salad with bright red cherry tomatoes and put a fresh daisy off to one side of the plate for a little asymmetry. (Please, don't eat the you-know-what.)

3 cucumbers
1 cup white vinegar
1 cup sugar
½ cup water
2 teaspoons salt (or to taste)
1 tablespoon chopped fresh dill
* or 1 teaspoon dried*
Freshly ground pepper

Peel the cucumbers and slice them in half lengthwise. Scrape out the seeds with a spoon. Cut each half in thirds horizontally and pare into attractive ovals. In a saucepan, combine the remaining ingredients and bring to a boil. Pour the mixture over the cucumber pieces in a 1-quart container. Cover tight and refrigerate.

Three to six servings.

❧ SPINACH–ONION–ORANGE SALAD

Attractive and colorful, this is good with chicken, fish and just about everything else.

10 ounces fresh spinach
2 oranges
1 small red onion, cut into rings

POPPY SEED DRESSING:

2 tablespoons honey or 2
   tablespoons sugar
½ cup cider vinegar or fresh
   lemon juice
1 tablespoon prepared mustard
2 tablespoons poppy seed
⅔ cup vegetable or corn oil
Salt
Freshly ground pepper

Pick over and remove the tough stems from the spinach; wash and dry. Tear the larger leaves into pieces, and leave the smaller leaves whole. Place the spinach in a 4-quart glass salad bowl. Peel the oranges and cut them into crosswise rings. Place the orange slices and the onion rings over the spinach. Just before serving, combine the ingredients for the dressing in a jar and shake well. Pour this over the salad and toss.

Four to six servings.

❧ BEEF SALAD PARISIENNE

1 ½ pounds lean boiled beef
2 cups sliced, boiled new potatoes
1 cup finely chopped green onions
2 cups chopped celery
3 sour pickles, chopped
¼ cup drained capers
1 cup green pepper strips (or mix
   green and red peppers)
6 tablespoons Basic Vinaigrette
   Dressing (p. 133)
Salt
Freshly ground pepper
2 eggs, hard cooked and chopped
Lettuce leaves

Cut beef into ½ inch cubes or julienne strips about ½ inch by 2 inches. Combine the potatoes, green onions, celery, beef, pickles, capers and green pepper strips and toss together in a 2½-quart serving bowl. Mix with the dressing, season to taste with salt and pepper and refrigerate for a few hours. Sprinkle with chopped egg and serve on lettuce leaves.

Six servings.

❧ BROCCOLI–CABBAGE SALAD

1 bunch broccoli
3 cups (½ pound) shredded
* cabbage*
1 cup shredded carrots (2 large
* carrots)*
1 package (10 ounces) frozen
* peas, thawed*

DRESSING:

½ cup salad oil
⅓ cup cider vinegar or lemon
* juice*
1 teaspoon grated onion
¾ teaspoon paprika
1 teaspoon celery seed
1 teaspoon dry mustard
2 tablespoons honey or sugar
½ cup evaporated milk
Salt
Freshly ground pepper

Trim the broccoli; cut off the flowerets and reserve. Peel the stems and cut them into 1-inch pieces. Toss the stems into boiling, salted water and cook until just crisp-tender. Add the flowerets and cook for 1 minute, no more. Drain immediately in a colander and run under cold water to stop the cooking. Drain well and dry with paper towels. Toss with the other vegetables. Mix the ingredients for the dressing in a jar. Shake well and toss with the vegetable mixture. Serve at room temperature.

Eight to ten servings.

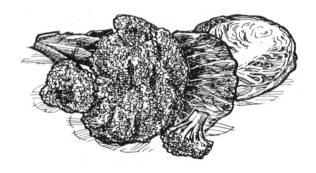

❧ ZUCCHINI SALAD

2 to 3 cloves garlic, halved
1 tablespoon olive oil
8 cups shredded raw zucchini
¾ cup chopped green onion,
* including some of the tops*
¼ cup Basic Vinaigrette
* Dressing (p. 133)*
Salt
Freshly ground pepper
2 teaspoons chopped fresh
* marjoram or thyme (optional)*

In a 10-inch skillet, sauté the garlic in oil until it begins to color; discard the garlic. Add the zucchini and green onions, cover and steam over moderate heat until just tender. Toss with the dressing, adding salt, pepper and fresh herbs if you have some at hand. Chill before serving.

Six to eight servings.

❧ CHICKEN SALAD VÉRONIQUE

This is wonderfully elegant way to use leftover chicken, but I like this salad so much, I often poach chicken breasts just for this purpose. It's especially appealing on the picnic table on a hot summer day, each serving crowned with a small bunch of grapes.

1 cup cubed red apple (unpeeled)
1 tablespoon fresh lemon juice
3 cups cubed cooked chicken
   (about 1 pound)
1 ¼ cups sliced celery
1 ¼ cups halved green grapes,
   seeded
½ cup pecan halves
⅓ cup dark raisins

DRESSING:

  ¾ cup mayonnaise
  ½ teaspoon salt (or to taste)
  ¼ teaspoon freshly ground
    pepper
  ¼ teaspoon dry mustard
  ½ teaspoon sugar
  1 teaspoon cider vinegar

In a large serving bowl, sprinkle the apple cubes with the lemon juice. Toss, then add the chicken, celery, grapes, pecans and raisins. Mix the dressing ingredients together, and stir this into the salad. Refrigerate for a few hours before serving.

Four to six servings.

❧ HOT POTATO SALAD

Good German bratwurst, hot potato salad and a crisp green salad—one of my favorite Sunday suppers. Vary the flavor by substituting Dijon-style mustard. And what a good way to use leftover potatoes!

DRESSING:

> 2 tablespoons wine or cider
>   vinegar
> 1 tablespoon prepared mustard
> 1 teaspoon Worcestershire
>   sauce
> Freshly ground pepper
> 1 teaspoon mustard seed

4 slices bacon
1 cup chopped onion
⅓ cup chopped green pepper
3 cups cubed potatoes (about 6
   medium potatoes), cooked
¼ cup chopped pimiento
4 eggs, hard cooked and sliced

Mix the dressing ingredients together and set aside. Fry the bacon in a 10-inch skillet until crisp; remove from the skillet, drain on paper towels and crumble. Keep enough of the bacon drippings to coat the bottom of the pan. Sauté the onion and green pepper until soft. Add the potatoes, pimiento, bacon and dressing, and mix gently until thoroughly warm. Garnish with the eggs and serve from the skillet.

Eight servings.

❧ RICE SALAD

1 cup cooked rice
½ cup chopped, drained cooked
   beets
½ cup chopped or shredded
   radishes
½ cup chopped celery
¼ cup drained capers
½ cup chopped green onions
¼ cup chopped pitted black or
   green olives
¼ to ½ cup Basic Vinaigrette
Dressing (p. 133)

Toss everything together and refrigerate or let stand for at least 2 hours. Serve at room temperature.

Six servings.

❧ TABOULI SALAD WITH WALNUTS

Be sure to prepare this at least 3 hours before serving. It needs time for the flavors to blend.

1 cup uncooked bulgur wheat
1 cup boiling water
Salt
¼ cup fresh lemon juice
1 clove garlic, minced
½ cup chopped green onions, including some of the tops
¼ cup olive oil
Freshly ground pepper
2 medium ripe tomatoes, peeled, seeded and diced
½ cup chopped fresh parsley
¼ cup chopped fresh mint or 2 tablespoons dried
½ cup coarsely grated carrot
1 green pepper, chopped
½ cup chopped walnuts
1 cucumber, peeled, seeded and chopped

Combine the bulgur, water and salt in a mixing bowl. Cover, and let stand for 10 to 15 minutes or until the bulgur is chewable; drain. Add the lemon juice, garlic, green onions, oil and pepper and mix thoroughly. Refrigerate for 2 to 3 hours. Just before serving, add the remaining ingredients and mix gently.

Six to eight servings.

❧ LENTIL SALAD

Try this with Leg of Lamb with Rosemary (p. 53); lentils and lamb are a classic combination.

1 cup cooked lentils
¼ cup chopped fresh parsley
Salt
Freshly ground pepper
¼ cup chopped celery
¼ cup chopped onion
¼ cup Basic Vinaigrette Dressing (p. 133)

Toss everything together and refrigerate or let stand for at least 2 hours. Taste and add more vinegar if it seems to need it. Serve at room temperature.

Two to three servings.

❧ LAMB SALADE NIÇOISE

Lamb is a real favorite of mine, but what to do with those leftovers you hate to throw away once you've served your roast, chops or stew? Here's the perfect meal-in-a-salad solution. It's also versatile, and open to substitutions —broccoli instead of green beans, for example. (If you substitute tuna and anchovies for the lamb, you'll have a more traditional Salade Niçoise.)

½ *pound green beans, cut into*
   2-inch lengths
1 head romaine lettuce
6 cooked new potatoes, sliced
1 cup Basic Vinaigrette Dressing
   (p. 133)
2 cups cooked lamb, cut into
   2-inch pencil-thin strips
1 cucumber, seeded and cut into
   2-inch pencil-thin strips
1 tablespoon finely chopped red
   pepper or pimiento
3 eggs, hard cooked and sliced
6 to 10 pitted black olives, sliced
4 to 5 firm, ripe tomatoes, sliced,
   or 1 pint cherry tomatoes
1 small red onion, cut into rings
2 small heads lettuce (Boston,
   bibb or red leaf)
1 bunch watercress

Plunge the green beans into boiling water and cook for 4 to 5 minutes or until crisp-tender; hold them in cold water until ready to use. Arrange the romaine leaves in a spokelike fashion in the bottom of a 10-inch quiche dish. Sprinkle the potatoes with a little of the dressing and arrange the slices upright around the rim of the dish. Place the lamb and cucumber strips in a dish and toss with about *3 tablespoons* of the dressing. Mentally dividing the quiche dish into quarters, fill the first quarter with the meat-cucumber mixture. Drain the green beans, mix them with the red pepper or pimiento and put the mixture into the second quarter. Put the hard-cooked eggs and black olives in the third quarter. Fill the fourth quarter with the tomatoes and onion rings. Drizzle a little dressing over all; put the remaining dressing in a serving bowl. Tear the small heads of lettuce into manageable pieces and mix with the watercress in a separate bowl. Ask each guest to take a helping of lettuce on a plate and to top it with a selection from the serving platter. Pass the dressing on the side.

Six servings.

BREADS, CAKES
and COOKIES

❧ FRENCH BREAD GLAZED WITH CHEESE

Don't hesitate to use a variety of cheeses in this way. It's an especially good use for Brie or other soft cheeses that have hung around too long and begun to dry out.

1 loaf French bread
½ pound (2 sticks) butter
2 cloves garlic, minced
2 teaspoons chopped fresh
   rosemary or 1 teaspoon dried
Freshly ground pepper
1 cup grated Swiss and/or
   Cheddar cheese

Cut the bread into ½-inch-thick slices. Melt the butter and add the garlic, rosemary and pepper. Dribble over the bread. Top with the cheese. Run under the broiler until the cheese is golden and bubbly.

Eight to ten servings.

❧ CHEESE WAFERS

Nice as an appetizer or snack. To vary these, try sprinkling the roll with sesame, poppy or caraway seed.

4 tablespoons (½ stick) butter,
   softened
½ pound Cheddar cheese, grated
¼ cup finely chopped green
   onions
½ teaspoon Worcestershire sauce
1 teaspoon prepared mustard
½ teaspoon salt
¾ cup flour

Mix all the ingredients together and form into a roll about 1½ inches in diameter. Chill for about 1 hour. Preheat the oven to 450° F. Slice into ⅓-inch slices. Bake for 12 to 15 minutes on an ungreased cookie sheet. Serve warm.

Three dozen wafers.

❧ RYE BISCUITS

One teaspoon dried dill or 2 teaspoons chopped fresh dill may be substituted for caraway seed. These should be served warm! They are marvelous with corned beef.

1 ¼ cups white flour
¾ cup rye flour
3 teaspoons baking powder
½ teaspoon salt
1 teaspoon caraway seed
4 tablespoons (½ stick) butter, chilled
1 tablespoon molasses
1 cup milk

Preheat the oven to 400° F. Mix the flours, baking powder, salt and caraway seed together. Using 2 knives, a food processor or your fingers, work the cold butter into the flour mixture to form small grains. Mix together the molasses and *¾ cup* of the milk and add this to the first mixture, just enough to form a stiff dough. Place the dough on a floured surface and work it into a rectangle about 1 inch thick. Cut with a floured biscuit cutter or simply cut into small squares. Place the biscuits on an ungreased cookie sheet. Brush the tops with the remaining ¼ cup of milk (to help them brown) and bake for about 10 minutes. Serve warm.

Eighteen biscuits.

❧ HERB BISCUITS

These make great accompaniments for soups—or almost any entrée. Try them also as a base for Chicken Livers Sauté (p. 68).

2 cups flour
2 ½ teaspoons baking powder
1 teaspoon salt
5 ⅓ tablespoons butter
2 tablespoons chopped fresh chives
1 tablespoon chopped fresh parsley
1 tablespoon chopped fresh dill, watercress or other herb
1 teaspoon grated lemon peel (yellow part only)
½ teaspoon freshly ground pepper
About ⅔ cup milk

Preheat the oven to 425° F. Mix the flour, baking powder and salt in a large bowl. Work in the butter with 2 knives, a pastry blender or your fingers, or do it in a food processor, until the mixture is like cornmeal. Add the herbs, lemon peel and pepper. Add the milk, stirring gently with a fork and using only enough to make the dough soft but not sticky. Knead on a lightly floured surface until smooth (about 25 strokes). Roll out the dough to a thickness of about ½ inch. Cut with a floured biscuit cutter or knife and put the biscuits on an ungreased baking sheet 1 inch apart. Bake for 12 to 15 minutes or until golden brown. Serve warm.

Eighteen biscuits.

❧ BLUEBERRY–CORN MUFFINS

These are moist and delicious as is, but just as good with 1 cup of grated unpeeled apple instead of the blueberries (think how attractive the tiny red flecks will look).

⅔ cup cornmeal
1 ⅓ cups flour
3 teaspoons baking powder
½ teaspoon salt
2 eggs
⅓ cup honey or ½ cup sugar
⅓ cup butter, melted
1 cup fresh blueberries
2 tablespoons sugar mixed with 1 teaspoon powdered cinnamon

Preheat the oven to 425° F. Combine the cornmeal, flour, baking powder and salt in a bowl. Lightly fold in the eggs, honey and melted butter. Fold in the blueberries. Turn into well-greased muffin tins, filling each cup about two-thirds full. Sprinkle some of the sugar-cinnamon mixture on each muffin. Bake for 20 to 25 minutes or until a toothpick inserted in the center of a muffin comes out clean.

Fourteen muffins.

❧ GINGERBREAD WITH BOILED CIDER GLAZE

¼ *pound (1 stick) butter, melted*
½ *cup sugar*
1 egg
¾ *cup dark molasses*
½ *cup apple cider*
½ *cup plain yogurt*
2 ¼ *cups flour*
½ *teaspoon salt*
1 teaspoon baking soda
1 teaspoon powdered ginger
1 teaspoon powdered cinnamon

GLAZE:

2 cups apple cider
1 stick cinnamon (optional)

1 cup heavy cream, whipped
Dusting of nutmeg

Preheat the oven to 325° F. In a large mixing bowl, combine the butter, sugar and egg. Blend in the molasses, cider and yogurt. In a separate mixing bowl, combine the flour, salt, baking soda, ginger and cinnamon; add this to the butter mixture and combine well to form a batter. Pour the batter into a buttered 8-inch cake pan and smooth the top with a rubber spatula. Bake for 1 ¼ hours or until a toothpick inserted in the center comes out clean.

While the cake bakes, make the glaze by bringing the cider (and cinnamon stick) to a boil in a heavy saucepan. Boil until the glaze is reduced to ½ cup and has a syrupy consistency. Spoon evenly over the *warm* cake. Let cool or serve warm. Pass a separate bowl of whipped cream, dusted with nutmeg if you like.

Sixteen squares.

❧ SCOTCH WHISKEY BREAD

You can substitute bourbon or rye if you prefer them to Scotch. Use half whole-wheat flour for a richer, firmer texture.

¾ cup raisins
¼ cup Scotch whiskey
4 cups flour
1 teaspoon salt
3 teaspoons baking powder
1 teaspoon baking soda
½ cup sugar
¼ pound (1 stick) butter, melted
2 eggs, lightly beaten
About 1 ½ cups milk

WHISKEY GLAZE:

1 cup confectioners' sugar
Drop of vanilla extract
About 1 ½ ounces Scotch
*   whiskey*

Preheat the oven to 350° F. Marinate the raisins in the Scotch for 30 minutes or heat them gently for 5 minutes. In a large mixing bowl, combine the flour, salt, baking powder, baking soda and sugar; add melted butter and raisin-whiskey mixture. In a small mixing bowl, add the beaten eggs to the milk. Pour this into the flour mixture and stir well, adding a little more milk if the batter is *very* thick. Pour the batter into 2 greased 1-quart soufflé dishes and bake for 1 hour or until a toothpick inserted in the center comes out clean. While it cools, mix the ingredients for the glaze together; the consistency will be runny. Dribble the loaves with the glaze.

Two loaves, four to five servings each.

•❧• PUMPKIN BREAD

Here's a pumpkin recipe that's easier than pie—a golden, moist bread that's great for Halloween goblins!

¼ cup vegetable or corn oil
4 tablespoons (½ stick) butter,
  melted
¾ cup sugar
1 egg
1 cup canned pumpkin puree
1 cup finely chopped apple
  (unpeeled)
2 cups flour
1 teaspoon baking soda
½ teaspoon baking powder
¼ teaspoon salt
½ teaspoon powdered cinnamon

TOPPING:

  2 tablespoons butter
  2 tablespoons sugar
  6 tablespoons flour
  1 teaspoon powdered cinnamon

Preheat the oven to 350° F. Using an electric or hand beater, mix together the oil, butter, sugar, egg, pumpkin puree and apple. Combine the dry ingredients and add them to the pumpkin mixture; mix until well moistened. Pour the batter into a 9-by-5-by-3-inch buttered loaf pan. Work the ingredients for the topping with your fingers until the mixture resembles coarse meal. Sprinkle this on top of the loaf. Bake for 1 hour. Let cool on a rack.

Six to eight servings.

ZUCCHINI BREAD

Zucchini is plentiful any time of the year, and this recipe puts it to delicious use.

3 eggs, lightly beaten
¼ pound (1 stick) butter, melted
½ cup sour cream
½ cup plain yogurt
¾ cup sugar
2 cups grated zucchini (unpeeled)
2 tablespoons maple syrup
1 ½ cups white flour
1 cup whole-wheat flour
1 teaspoon baking powder
1 teaspoon baking soda
1 teaspoon salt
1 teaspoon powdered cinnamon
¼ teaspoon powdered allspice
⅔ cup currants or raisins
⅔ cup chopped walnuts

Preheat the oven to 350° F. Mix the eggs, butter, sour cream, yogurt, sugar, zucchini and maple syrup together; set aside. Mix the remaining ingredients together and, using a wooden spoon or an electric beater, combine the zucchini mixture with the flour mixture. Add the currants and nuts and mix well. Spoon into 2 well-buttered 8½-by-4½-inch loaf pans. Bake for about 55 minutes. Let cool for 10 minutes before removing from the pans.

Two loaves.

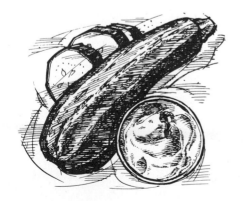

❀ POUND SPONGE CAKE

A cross between two great basic cakes, this is the perfect "plain cake" to eat by itself or with all kinds of embellishments, such as fruit, chocolate sauce, ice cream or . . . whatever you have fantasies about.

1 ½ cups sugar
1 ½ sticks unsalted butter,
  softened
6 eggs, separated
1 ½ cups flour
1 ½ teaspoons salt
1 ½ teaspoons baking powder
1 ½ teaspoons vanilla extract

Preheat the oven to 325° F. Cream the sugar and butter together until fluffy. Add the egg yolks, beating after each addition. Combine the flour, salt and baking powder and gradually add to the creamed mixture. Beat in the vanilla. In a separate bowl, beat the egg whites until they form soft peaks; fold this into the other mixture. Pour the batter into a buttered 2-quart ring mold. Bake for 45 to 50 minutes or until a toothpick inserted in the center comes out clean. Serve with fresh fruit or enjoy it plain.

Six or more servings.

STRAWBERRY SHORTCAKES

You should have 8 nice individual serving dishes for this cake.

2 cups flour
4 teaspoons baking powder
½ teaspoon salt
¼ cup sugar
¼ pound (1 stick) butter, chilled
* and cut into small pieces*
¾ cup milk

TOPPING:

1 cup sugar
2 quarts fresh strawberries,
* sliced*
1 cup heavy cream

Preheat the oven to 450° F. Mix the flour, baking powder, salt and sugar. Using 2 knives, a pastry blender, a food processor or your fingers, work in the butter until texture is like cornmeal. Pour in the milk and mix very quickly. Place on a generously floured surface, pat into an 8-inch square that is ½-inch thick. Cut into sixteen 2-inch squares and place on ungreased baking sheet (touching each other for soft sides; set apart for crusty sides). Bake for 12 to 15 minutes. Place 2 biscuits in each serving bowl, then prepare the topping by sprinkling the sugar over the strawberries and spooning them over the biscuits (or use as a filling between the 2 biscuits). Whip the cream and spoon some over each.

Eight servings.

❦ BANANA UPSIDE-DOWN CAKE

As this recipe proves, pineapple isn't the only food that works well upside down.

9 ½ tablespoons butter
½ cup brown sugar
1 ½ cups granulated white sugar
1 cup mashed bananas (about 2 bananas)
2 eggs
1 tablespoon vanilla extract
¼ cup dark rum
2 cups flour
1 teaspoon baking soda
½ teaspoon salt
1 teaspoon powdered cinnamon
½ teaspoon nutmeg
¼ teaspoon powdered ginger
½ cup sour cream
2 large unripe bananas, cut into ⅓-inch slices
1 ¼ cups broken walnuts

Preheat the oven to 350° F. In a 10-inch oven-proof skillet, melt 5 ½ tablespoons of the butter with the brown sugar over very low heat. Meanwhile, in a large mixing bowl, cream the remaining 4 tablespoons butter with the white sugar until light. Add the mashed bananas, eggs, vanilla and rum; stir. Then add the flour, baking soda, salt and spices; beat in the sour cream. Arrange the banana slices in a pretty pattern in the skillet with the brown sugar mixture; top with the walnuts. Pour the batter over all and place in the oven for 50 to 60 minutes or until a toothpick inserted in the center comes out clean. Turn out immediately onto a plate. Serve with ice cream if you're feeling especially sinful.

Eight to ten servings.

HERB BISCUITS *and* BLUEBERRY-CORN BISCUITS

MELANGE OF FRUITS

◦❁◦ POUND SPONGE CAKE

◦❁◦ FROZEN YOGURT FRUIT PIE *and* LEMON MOUSSE

(L to R)
FILLED OATMEAL BARS, WALNUT BROWNIES, TOFFEE COOKIES
and PUMPKIN BREAD

STRAWBERRY SHORTCAKES

❧ WALNUT CAKE

Serve this versatile cake with applesauce, whipped cream, ice cream or Quick Zabaglione Sauce (p. 171).

4 tablespoons (½ stick) butter, softened
1 egg
⅓ cup sugar
2 tablespoons grated lemon peel (yellow part only; about 2 lemons)
1 teaspoon baking powder
¾ cup flour
1 cup chopped walnuts
Confectioners' sugar

Preheat the oven to 350° F. Blend the butter with an electric mixer, gradually adding the egg, sugar, lemon peel and baking powder. Fold in the flour and nuts. Pour the batter into a buttered 8-inch cake pan. Bake for 45 minutes. Either serve warm from the pan or turn out onto a serving platter and let cool. Dust with confectioners' sugar.

Six servings.

❧ APPLESAUCE SPICE CUPCAKES WITH TWO FROSTINGS

The chocolate glaze and the cream-cheese frosting are each wonderful, but these cupcakes are also good plain or simply dusted with confectioners' sugar. Try a few each way.

¼ pound (1 stick) butter
1 cup sugar
1 egg
1 cup applesauce
1 ¾ cups flour
1 teaspoon baking soda
1 teaspoon powdered cinnamon
1 teaspoon nutmeg
¼ teaspoon powdered cloves
½ teaspoon salt
½ cup chopped walnuts
Chocolate Glaze or *Cream Cheese Frosting (see below)*

Preheat the oven to 350° F. Using an electric beater, beat the butter and sugar together until creamy. Add the egg and beat until fluffy. Mix in the applesauce. In a separate, medium mixing bowl, combine the dry ingredients and stir into the applesauce mixture. Then add the walnuts and combine well. Spoon the batter into buttered muffin tins or small, heat-resistant glass custard cups, filling each cup ⅔ full. Bake for about 18 minutes or until a toothpick inserted in the center of a cupcake comes out clean. Let cool for about 5 minutes, then remove from the pan and brush the tops with Chocolate Glaze or Cream Cheese Frosting.

Eighteen cupcakes.

CHOCOLATE GLAZE:

⅓ cup semisweet chocolate morsels or *2 ounces semisweet chocolate*
2 tablespoons light corn syrup
1 teaspoon hot water

Melt the chocolate in the top of a double boiler over boiling water. Remove from the heat, add the corn syrup and water and stir until smooth. Spread the glaze on the cupcakes with a knife while still warm.

CREAM CHEESE FROSTING:

3 ounces cream cheese, softened
1 to 2 tablespoons milk
¾ cup confectioners' sugar, sifted
1 teaspoon vanilla extract
1 teaspoon grated orange peel (optional)
Dash of powdered cinnamon (optional)
Dash of nutmeg (optional)

Beat the cream cheese and milk together until fluffy. Gradually add the sugar and blend. Add the vanilla and mix well. Mix in grated orange peel, cinnamon or nutmeg for extra flavor if you wish.

❀ WALNUT BROWNIES

Be careful not to overcook these brownies. They should be slightly moist and chewy.

4 tablespoons (½ stick) butter
4 ounces unsweetened chocolate
1 cup sugar
2 eggs, lightly beaten
1 ½ teaspoons vanilla extract
1 cup flour
¼ teaspoon salt
½ cup sour cream
⅔ cup chopped walnuts

Preheat the oven to 350° F. Melt the butter with the chocolate in the top of a double boiler over hot water. In a 1½-quart mixing bowl, beat the sugar into the eggs, then slowly beat in the melted chocolate mixture. Stir in the vanilla. Add the flour, 2 tablespoonfuls at a time, mixing well after each addition. Stir in the salt, sour cream and walnuts. Spoon into a buttered 8-inch-square pan and bake for 20 to 25 minutes. Let cool and cut into squares.

Twenty-four brownies.

❀ FILLED OATMEAL BARS

1 ½ cups flour
1 teaspoon baking powder
½ teaspoon salt
1 ½ cups rolled oats
1 teaspoon grated orange peel
1 cup brown sugar
¾ cup butter (1 ½ sticks), chilled and cut into small pieces
1 cup strawberry preserves, apple butter, orange marmalade or blueberry jam

Preheat the oven to 350° F. Mix the flour, baking powder, salt, oats, orange peel and sugar. Add the butter, working it into the flour mixture with your fingers, a pastry blender, 2 knives or a food processor until it looks like coarse cornmeal. Press half the mixture into a well-buttered 8-inch-square pan. Spread with jam, then top with the remaining batter. Bake for 40 minutes. Let cool, then cut into 2-by-1-inch bars.

Thirty-two bars.

❧ REFRIGERATOR BUTTER COOKIES

Make the dough for these cookies at least 8 hours before you want to bake them so that it can chill thoroughly. The unbaked dough will keep well in the refrigerator, wrapped in foil or wax paper, for about a week. You can slice off whatever amount you need and save the rest for another time. You can also freeze the unused dough. Try changing the personality of these cookies by pressing a chocolate chip or an almond half into the center of each cookie slice before baking or by rolling the edges of a section of the dough in finely chopped nuts or a cinnamon-sugar mixture before slicing the dough into cookies.

½ pound (2 sticks) butter,
  softened
1 ⅓ cups sugar
2 eggs
1 teaspoon vanilla extract
½ teaspoon almond extract
2 ¾ cups flour
½ teaspoon baking soda
1 teaspoon salt

Using an electric beater, beat the butter until light and fluffy, then beat in the sugar, eggs, vanilla and almond extract. In a separate medium mixing bowl, combine the dry ingredients, and add them to the butter mixture. Shape the dough with your hands into a long roll, about 2½ inches in diameter. Wrap in foil or waxed paper and refrigerate overnight. When ready to bake, preheat the oven to 400° F. Slice the dough into thin cookie slices (½-inch thick for chewy cookies, thinner for crispy cookies) and set slightly apart on ungreased cookie sheets. Bake for 6 to 8 minutes or until just browned on the rims.

Three dozen cookies.

❧ TOFFEE COOKIES

½ pound (2 sticks) butter,
  softened
1 cup sugar
1 egg, separated
1 teaspoon powdered cinnamon
2 cups flour
½ cup chopped pecans

Preheat the oven to 350° F. Using an electric beater, cream the the butter, then add the sugar, beating well. Add the egg yolk, then gradually add the cinnamon and flour, mixing well. Spread the dough very thin on a lightly greased cookie sheet (it should cover most of the sheet). Spread with slightly beaten egg white and the chopped pecans. Bake until golden brown, about 40 to 45 minutes, watching carefully so that it doesn't burn. Cut while still warm.

Three dozen cookies.

DESSERTS

❧ MÉLANGE OF FRUITS

4 cups fresh fruit*

DRESSING:

½ cup dry white wine
¼ cup honey
¼ teaspoon powdered
   cinnamon
Dash of powdered allspice
Dash of Amaretto or other
   sweet liqueur (optional)

3 tablespoons chopped fresh mint

Place the fruit in a 1½-quart serving bowl. Mix the dressing ingredients together until honey dissolves. Pour over the fruit and refrigerate for several hours. Sprinkle with mint before serving.

Four servings.

---

*This can be any combination of raspberries, strawberries, oranges (peeled and sliced or sectioned), green seedless grapes, melon balls, peaches (peeled and cut into wedges) or pears (peeled and sliced).

❧ LAYERED FRUIT COMPOTE

2 large Valencia or temple
   oranges
3 ripe bananas
¼ cup confectioners' sugar
1 cup shredded coconut

Peel the oranges and bananas and cut them into thin round slices. Arrange a layer of sliced oranges in individual serving dishes or in a large bowl. Mix the sugar and coconut together and sprinkle some on top. Arrange a second layer of bananas on top and sprinkle with the coconut mixture. Continue to alternate layers, sprinkling with sugared coconut, until all the fruit is used. Top with the remaining coconut mixture. Chill before serving.

Four servings.

❧ HOT FRUIT COMPOTE

Use any combination of fruits here, depending on what is available. Serve with small slices of Pound Sponge Cake (p. 150).

1 cup cider or apple juice
¼ cup honey
1 stick cinnamon
½ pound fresh pineapple or 1 can (8 ounces) unsweetened pineapple chunks, drained
2 oranges, peeled and cut into wedges
2 apples, cored and cut into wedges
1 can Bing cherries, drained
2 teaspoons minced gingerroot or ¼ teaspoon powdered ginger

Cook the cider, honey and cinnamon together in a 2½-quart saucepan until slightly thickened. If you are using fresh pineapple, cut it into 1-inch cubes. Add the pineapple, oranges, apples and cherries. Cover, and cook gently for about 15 minutes. Remove the cinnamon stick and add the ginger. Serve warm.

Four servings.

❧ APPLE CRUMB DESSERT

4 cups sliced apples (peeled)
1 to 2 tablespoons fresh lemon juice
Powdered cinnamon, nutmeg or cardamom
1 cup flour
1 cup sugar
Pinch of salt
1 teaspoon baking powder
1 egg
4 tablespoons (½ stick) butter, melted

Preheat the oven to 350° F. Arrange the sliced apples in a 9-inch pie plate or an 8-inch-square cake pan. Sprinkle with the lemon juice and spice. In a medium mixing bowl, combine the flour, sugar, salt and baking powder; break the egg into the flour mixture and mix lightly with a fork. Sprinkle over the apples, pour the butter over them and bake for 30 minutes. Serve either warm or cold.

Six servings.

❧ APPLE–CRANBERRY FRITTATA

This skillet dessert is especially nice at Sunday brunch. You can use pears or peaches instead of apples if you wish.

2 tablespoons butter
1 ½ cups thinly sliced apples
   (peeled)
2 tablespoons fresh lemon juice
⅔ cup whole cranberry sauce
1 tablespoon grated orange peel
8 eggs, lightly beaten
2 tablespoons flour
Pinch of salt

TOPPING:

  ½ cup walnut pieces
  2 tablespoons mixed cinnamon
   and sugar

Preheat the oven to 350° F. Melt the butter in a 10-inch ovenproof skillet. Add the apples, lemon juice and cranberry sauce and cook over low heat until the apples are tender but not mushy (5 minutes at most). Mix together the remaining ingredients and pour over the apples. Stir gently with a fork until blended. Sprinkle with the topping ingredients and bake until the eggs are set and the topping is browned, about 25 to 30 minutes. Serve either hot or at room temperature.

Six servings.

❧ POACHED APPLES IN CITRUS SAUCE

Serve these by themselves, as a pleasantly tart topping for pudding and leftover cake, or as a base for ice cream or whipped cream. You'll think of many other uses yourself!

8 apples, peeled, cored and
   quartered
Juice of 1 lemon
Juice of 1 orange
Grated peel of 1 lemon (yellow
   part only)
Grated peel of 1 orange (orange
   part only)
4 tablespoons (½ stick) butter
¼ cup brown sugar

Sprinkle the quartered apples with lemon juice to prevent discoloring. Mix with remaining ingredients in a 2½-quart saucepan and cook, covered, over low heat for 15 minutes. Check frequently and do not overcook. Remove the apples with a slotted spoon. Uncover and reduce the juices, stirring often, until the syrup is thick. Pour the syrup over the apples and serve either warm or cool.

Six to eight servings.

❦ BANANAS FLAMBÉ

This is one of my most successful "grand finales"; it looks dramatic and tastes so good!

4 firm, ripe bananas
4 tablespoons (½ stick) butter
4 teaspoons brown sugar
½ cup cognac

Slice the bananas very thin. In an 8½-inch skillet, sauté them quickly in the butter, sprinkling them with the brown sugar so that they caramelize a little. Warm the cognac in a small saucepan. Pour the warm cognac over the bananas, and *carefully standing well back, with any venting fan turned off,* strike a match and light the cognac in the pan, shaking the pan until the flame dies down. Serve directly from the pan, or over pound cake or ice cream, with or without whipped cream.

Four servings.

Variations:

- Add 2 to 4 tablespoons of your favorite chopped nut (pecans, walnuts, hazelnuts, almonds) and/or a tablespoon of grated lemon, lime or orange peel.
- Use fresh peaches or pears instead of bananas.
- Use rum instead of cognac.

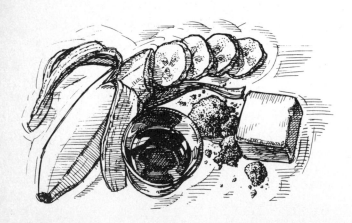

❧ STRAWBERRY BANANA

If you're fortunate enough to have fresh raspberries (black or red) or blueberries, you may substitute them for the strawberries. You'll have to change the name of the dish, too.

1 quart strawberries, hulled and sliced
2 tablespoons granulated sugar
½ teaspoon orange extract
1 banana
1 tablespoon confectioners' sugar
¼ teaspoon nutmeg
1 cup heavy cream

Mash a few (6 to 8) of the berries with a fork and add them to the whole berries. Sprinkle with granulated sugar and orange extract; chill. Puree the banana, confectioners' sugar and nutmeg in a blender or food processor. Whip the cream until stiff, then fold in the banana mixture. Spoon into individual serving dishes. Top with the strawberry mixture.

Six to eight servings.

❧ BROILED GRAPEFRUIT WITH AMARETTO

A pleasing and unusual combination. Garnish with fresh mint sprigs or fresh cherries if you have some. Italian Amaretti cookies or macaroons are a natural accompaniment.

3 grapefruit
2 tablespoons Amaretto liqueur
3 tablespoons brown sugar
3 tablespoons slivered almonds

Preheat the oven for broiling. Slice the grapefruit into halves and remove the seeds. Cut around the edges and between the sections to loosen them, then cut out the tough, fibrous center, using a scissors or corer. Sprinkle each half with 1 teaspoon Amaretto, ½ tablespoon brown sugar, and ½ tablespoon slivered almonds. Place the grapefruit halves in a 9-by-13-inch oblong broilerproof pan. Broil the grapefruit until the juice bubbles and the edges of peels are slightly browned, about 5 to 10 minutes. Serve hot.

Six servings.

✿ GRAPEFRUIT GRANITA

One of the most refreshing summer desserts I know! Use pink grapefruit if possible, and don't forget to save the shells.

1 cup sugar
2 cups water
Juice of 8 to 10 grapefruit or 1 ½ quarts grapefruit juice
¼ cup fresh lemon juice
Yellow peel of 1 lemon, diced small
8 to 10 fresh cherries

Cook the sugar and water for 10 minutes in a 2½-quart saucepan. Stir in the grapefruit and lemon juices and the lemon peel. Pour into ice trays and freeze, stirring now and then. Empty the trays into a food processor with the steel blade on, and, using an on-off motion, blend until the granita is an icy mush. Spoon into hollowed-out grapefruit halves or frosted goblets, and keep in the freezer until ready to serve. Top each with a fresh cherry.

Four to eight servings.

✿ PEACHY CREPES

Add a dash of Cointreau to the peaches for a special touch.

8 crepes (p. 64)
6 firm, slightly underripe peaches
1 tablespoon butter
½ cup orange juice
¼ cup orange marmalade

Preheat the oven to 350° F. Prepare the crepes and set aside. Put the peaches in boiling water for 1 minute to loosen their skins; peel them and cut them into thick slices. Melt the butter in a 10-inch skillet and add the orange juice and marmalade. Add the peaches and cook, stirring gently, until they are just soft (but still firm and holding their shape) and the liquid has thickened. Spoon the peaches into the crepes and roll them. Place the filled crepes, seam side *down,* on an ovenproof serving dish. Spoon the pan juices on top and warm briefly in the oven. Serve as is or with vanilla ice cream, whipped cream or yogurt.

Four servings.

LEMON MOUSSE

Light and delicate. I usually serve this after a heavy meal. Fresh mint sprigs make a nice garnish, or top with fresh red raspberries when they're in season.

4 eggs, separated
1 cup sugar
½ cup fresh lemon juice
1 ½ packets unflavored gelatin
⅓ cup cold water
Yellow peel of 1 lemon, grated
1 teaspoon vanilla extract
Pinch of salt
1 ½ cups heavy cream

Place the egg yolks, *½ cup* of the sugar and the lemon juice in the top of a double boiler over simmering water. Cook for 5 minutes, stirring, until hot but not boiling. Soften the gelatin in the water. Add the gelatin to the egg-lemon mixture, stirring well until dissolved. Add the lemon peel, vanilla and salt; mix thoroughly and pour into a bowl to cool. Beat the egg whites. As they get foamy and thicken slightly, gradually add the remaining *½ cup* sugar. Beat until soft peaks form, then fold into the egg-lemon mixture. Beat the cream at medium speed until it becomes quite thick but not stiff. Pour the lemon mixture into the cream and fold it in thoroughly. Pour into a 2-quart soufflé dish. Chill for several hours before serving.

Six to eight servings.

Variation:

Substitute lime juice and lime peel for lemon, and rum (either extract or the real thing) for the vanilla.

❀ SPICED PEARS

Rich, beautiful and healthy, and easy to make!

2 cups cranberry juice or
Burgundy
1 stick cinnamon
6 whole cloves
⅓ cup honey
6 firm, ripe pears

In a 2½-quart saucepan, combine the cranberry juice or wine, spices and honey, and heat until hot and well mixed. Peel the pears, leaving the stems intact, and core them from the bottom, flattening the bottom a little so that they'll stand upright. Place the pears in the hot liquid. Bring to a boil, then simmer, covered, for about 15 to 20 minutes or until the pears are tender (test with a toothpick). While simmering, occasionally turn the pears in the liquid so that they are evenly coated. Remove the pears and place them upright on a serving dish. Spoon a little of the liquid over them. Reduce the remaining liquid by half by boiling over high heat. Let cool to room temperature and pour over the pears. Serve cool or at room temperature and, if you wish, add a dollop of whipped cream, plain yogurt or your favorite soft custard.

Six servings.

❀ PINEAPPLE PARFAIT

3 cups fresh crushed or canned
pineapple
2 cups shredded coconut
2 pints coffee ice cream

Layer the pineapple and shredded coconut alternately with coffee ice cream in six 8-ounce parfait glasses. Store in the freezer to mellow. Remove from the freezer at least 1 hour before serving.

Six servings.

❧ RHUBARB FOOL

Here's what to do when you feel like a fool. This always spells "spring" to me.

7 cups fresh rhubarb stems (no leaves)
1 cup crushed gingersnaps
⅔ cups sugar
½ teaspoon powdered cinnamon
3 tablespoons butter, melted
Whipped cream or vanilla ice cream

Preheat the oven to 350° F. Trim and cut the rhubarb into 1-inch pieces. Place in a large saucepan, cover and cook for about 10 minutes over medium-low heat, stirring often until just tender (not mushy); drain well. Combine the crushed gingersnaps with the sugar and cinnamon. Add the melted butter and mix well. Lightly grease a 1-quart casserole, add a layer of the drained rhubarb and sprinkle with some of the crumb mixture. Repeat the layering, ending with the crumbs. Bake for 15 minutes. Let cool slightly, but serve warm, topped with whipped cream or vanilla ice cream.

Six to eight servings.

❧ FRESH STRAWBERRIES PLUS

The pepper adds subtle interest. I use white or black pepper, always freshly ground.

1 quart fresh strawberries
2 tablespoons sugar (or to taste)
2 tablespoons orange juice
½ teaspoon grated orange peel
2 tablespoons Cointreau
¼ teaspoon freshly ground pepper

Wash the berries and sort them, putting the perfect ones in a 1-quart serving bowl. Mash the soft or mushy berries in a mixing bowl, adding the sugar, orange juice, orange peel, Cointreau and pepper. Pour over the berries and chill before serving.

Four to six servings.

❧ BERRY SHERBET

Here's an easy sherbet you can make with strawberries or raspberries.

*1 pint fresh strawberries or 2
cups unsweetened frozen
strawberries or raspberries,
thawed
1 ¼ cups sugar
7 tablespoons fresh lemon juice
2 cups water
½ cup light corn syrup
12 fresh strawberries
¼ cup kirsch*

Crush the strawberries; add ¼ *cup* of the sugar and 4 *tablespoons* of the lemon juice; set aside. Combine the water with the remaining *1 cup* sugar and the corn syrup in a saucepan. Stir over high heat until the sugar dissolves. When the mixture clears, boil for 5 minutes. Add the remaining *3 tablespoons* lemon juice and let cool thoroughly. Stir in the strawberry mixture. Pour into a large rectangular dish and cover. Freeze until firm. Remove from the freezer and cut into chunks. Beat in an electric mixer until smooth. Pour into a 1-quart serving bowl, cover well and refreeze. Top with fresh strawberries tossed in kirsch.

One quart.

❧ FROZEN STRAWBERRY MOUSSE

My own favorite strawberry recipe, stunning but easy to make, pleasantly spiked for grown-ups only.

*1 quart strawberries, hulled
¾ cup sugar
½ cup rosé wine
1 pint heavy cream
2 teaspoons vanilla extract
Whipped cream*

In a blender or food processor, combine the strawberries, sugar and wine; whirl until smooth. Pour into a bowl. Whip the cream until stiff, add the vanilla and fold into the strawberry mixture. Pour into a 2-quart soufflé dish. Cover with plastic wrap and freeze until hard. Thirty minutes before serving, turn out of the dish onto a platter by dipping the bottom into lukewarm water for a few seconds. Allow to stand in the refrigerator for 30 minutes before cutting into wedges to serve. Serve topped with whipped cream.

Six servings.

❧ FROZEN YOGURT FRUIT PIE

Here's a do-it-yourself recipe that's wonderfully wholesome. Pick a flavored yogurt that will mix with or match the fruit, and vary the flavorings as well. Some suggestions: banana yogurt over sliced bananas mixed with ¼ teaspoon rum extract; strawberry yogurt over fresh strawberries mixed with ¼ teaspoon orange extract.

CRUST:

  2 cups granola
  2 tablespoons butter, melted

FILLING:

  3 cups flavored yogurt
  1 to 2 tablespoons honey
  2 cups fruit, sliced or diced
  ¼ teaspoon flavored extract

Preheat the oven to 400° F. Pulverize the granola in a food processor or blender. Mix with the melted butter and press into a 9-inch pie plate. Bake for 10 minutes or until the crumbs are browned. Mix the yogurt with the honey, *1 cup* of the fruit and the extract. Pour the mixture into the baked crust. Top with the remaining *1 cup* fruit (it will partially sink into the pie). Cover with plastic wrap and freeze until firm. Thirty minutes before serving, place the pie in the refrigerator to soften slightly.

Serves six.

❧ CHOCOLATE PANCAKES

If you like chocolate *and* pancakes (and who doesn't?), here's a happy combination of good things! Allow three to six pancakes per serving depending on pancake size. Serve them topped with whipped cream and a sprinkling of freshly grated chocolate.

  4 tablespoons (½ stick) butter
  3 ounces semisweet chocolate
  1 ½ cups flour
  ⅓ cup sugar
  1 teaspoon baking soda
  ½ teaspoon salt
  ¼ teaspoon powdered cinnamon
  2 eggs, lightly beaten
  1 ½ cups milk

Combine the butter and chocolate in the top of a double boiler over boiling water and stir until melted. Combine the flour, sugar, baking soda, salt and cinnamon. Add the eggs and milk, and mix thoroughly. Add the butter-chocolate mixture and stir. Drop the batter from a tablespoon into a hot buttered 10-inch skillet. Cook until just crisp on one side, then turn and cook the other side. Serve warm.

Six to eight servings.

✤ LONI KUHN'S OMELETTE SOUFFLÉ FLAMBÉ

This is one of the most elegant and spectacular desserts imaginable, and very easy to prepare!

4 tablespoons (½ stick) butter
¾ cup plus 2 tablespoons
 granulated sugar
8 eggs, separated
⅜ cup brandy or rum
3 tablespoons grated lemon peel

Preheat the oven to 375° F. Warm a 10-inch skillet on top of the stove, remove from the heat and butter it thoroughly, including the sides. Sprinkle the bottom and sides with ¼ cup of the sugar; set aside. Beat the egg yolks until pale and lemon colored. Gradually beat in *½ cup* of the sugar and add *¼ cup* of the brandy or rum. Beat the egg whites until firm peaks are formed and fold ⅓ of them into the yolk mixture along with the lemon peel. Fold in the rest of the whites. Pour the mixture into the prepared skillet and place in the oven for about 20 minutes or until the soufflé is browned and firm. (Shake the skillet gently: The center of the soufflé should not jiggle.) Remove the soufflé from the oven and sprinkle evenly with the remaining *2 tablespoons* sugar. Warm the remaining *2 tablespoons* brandy or rum and pour it into a long-handled metal soup or gravy ladle. Ignite and sprinkle over the soufflé. Serve at once from the skillet.

Six servings.

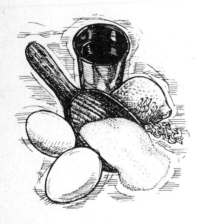

❧ FROZEN MINCEMEAT CREAM

This is a terrific dessert for the holiday season, but it's too good not to serve year-round! (You might try serving a small dash of this cream with a portion of pumpkin or apple pie for an unbeatable combination.)

1 cup prepared mincemeat
½ cup chopped pecans
1 tablespoon dark rum
1 cup heavy cream
Pecan halves

In a small mixing bowl, mix the mincemeat, pecans and rum. Whip the cream until just stiff and fold it into the mincemeat. Spoon the mixture into a 1-pint soufflé dish. Cover and freeze until hard. Garnish with pecan halves before serving.

Four servings.

❧ QUICK ZABAGLIONE SAUCE

You can serve this in a tall-stemmed glass or use it as a sauce over fruit. It *must* be made at the last moment, for it will collapse if it stands around for more than 10 or 15 minutes.

3 egg yolks
¼ cup sugar
⅓ cup Madeira or Marsala
*   wine*

Combine the egg yolks, sugar and Madeira wine in the top of a double boiler over *simmering,* not boiling, water. Beat with a portable electric mixer or a wire whisk until the mixture becomes thick and fluffy, expanding in volume. (This will take 5 to 6 minutes with the mixer, double that with the whisk.) Serve at once or spoon over cold fruit and serve.

Four servings; six when served over fruit.

❧ CHOCOLATE POTS DE CRÈME

A rich chocolate flavor, but not *too* sweet.

2 cups heavy cream
1 teaspoon sugar
4 ounces semisweet chocolate
3 egg yolks
Dash of salt
1 teaspoon vanilla extract
½ teaspoon grated orange peel
¼ teaspoon powdered cinnamon
About ½ cup crumbled almond macaroons or vanilla wafer crumbs (optional)

Preheat the oven to 325° F. Heat the cream and sugar in the top of a double boiler over boiling water, stirring until the sugar dissolves. Add the chocolate and melt, mixing well. Beat the egg yolks until light yellow. Pour the chocolate mixture over them gradually, beating well. Add the salt, vanilla, orange peel and cinnamon and mix well. Pour into four individual heatproof dishes or custard cups. Place the dishes in a pan of water. Bake for about 15 minutes. Let cool, then chill in the refrigerator. Before serving, sprinkle with cookie crumbs if you wish.

Four servings.

❧ MOCHA CREAM

Serve this in a 1-pint soufflé dish and top with whipped cream and grated chocolate for an extra flourish.

1 ½ ounces semisweet chocolate
¼ cup strong coffee, heated
½ cup sugar
3 egg yolks
½ cup heavy cream

Melt the chocolate in the hot coffee; add the sugar, stirring until it is dissolved. Place the mixture in a blender or food processor and add the egg yolks blending until smooth. In a small mixing bowl, beat the cream until stiff. Fold the chocolate mixture into the cream. Refrigerate until ready to serve.

Four servings.

CRÈME BRÛLÉE

This elegant, classic custard dessert is much easier to make than most people realize. But don't let your mind wander while it's under the broiler—a minute too long and the crème may burn!

4 eggs
¼ cup sugar
1 teaspoon cornstarch
1 pint heavy cream, scalded
1 teaspoon vanilla extract
½ cup superfine sugar (or granulated sugar pulverized in a food processor or blender)

Beat the eggs until thick and lemon colored. Mix the sugar and cornstarch and add this very gradually to the eggs. Gradually pour the scalded cream into the eggs, stirring constantly. Place the mixture in the top of a double boiler over simmering water and stir constantly until the mixture coats a wooden spoon, about 8 to 10 minutes. Remove from the heat immediately and stir in the vanilla. Pour into 4 broilerproof serving dishes, cover with foil or plastic wrap, let cool, then chill for 2 to 3 hours. Remove the wrap, cover with a heavy, even coating of superfine sugar and place in a large baking pan filled with ice and cold water (the water should come halfway up the sides of the dishes). Place under the preheated broiler, *watching constantly,* until the sugar melts and forms a caramel-brown coating, about 5 to 6 minutes. Hold in the refrigerator until serving time.

Four servings.

CINNAMON BREAD PUDDING

Serve this warm from the oven, perhaps with a dollop of vanilla ice cream.

8 slices stale cinnamon-raisin bread, buttered and diced
1 pint half-and-half
2 to 4 tablespoons rum (optional)
⅓ cup brown sugar
2 eggs, beaten
Pinch of nutmeg

Preheat the oven to 325° F. Combine all the ingredients and let soak for 10 to 15 minutes. Bake in a 1½-quart buttered casserole for 50 to 60 minutes.

Six to eight servings.

❧ Weekly Menu Planning

Now you've come to a really important part of this book. For what good are terrific recipes for soups, entrées, salads, vegetables, desserts and so forth, until you've made them part of well-planned menus, in which they "hang together" and complement one another? Take it one step further: Instead of planning for one day at a time, try to work out a series of interrelated menus to use over a period of days—even a week at a time—and take advantage of foods that are in season and therefore cheap and plentiful.

That's what I've done in this chapter, using recipes from this book to compile four weeks' of menus, one for each season of the year. Certain dishes are planned so that there will be leftovers to use in another meal: This makes marketing easier (fewer separate items on the list) and is a thrifty and creative way to cook.

In preparing the menus, I've tried to achieve a balance between light and heavy foods within each meal plan. I've also considered how the foods will look, either together or in sequence, trying to balance colors, textures and shapes.

But don't get trapped by *my* formulas; rules, after all, are meant to be broken. I've been known to serve a cold soup in February, plan a picnic in November and dish out a hearty stew in July. These menu plans are not meant to be followed to a T. They're really here to illustrate an approach to marketing and cooking that ultimately requires your *own* ingenuity. Break the rules! Change a seasoning, change an entire dish, take my advice or not —but have a happy, creative time in *your* kitchen! Cheers!

❧ SPRING MENUS

DAY 1

Leg of Lamb with Rosemary[1]
Dilled New Potatoes[2]
Asparagus Baked in Foil[2]

Rhubarb Fool

DAY 2

Chicken Hash[3]
Fluffy Buttered Rice[4]
Citrus Carrots[4]

Crème Brûlée

DAY 3

Grandma's Chicken Soup[3,4]
Cheese Wafers
Lamb Salade Niçoise[1,2]

Grapefruit Granita

DAY 4

Fish Fillets with Spinach[5]
Mashed Potatoes with Green
    Onions

Bananas Flambé[6]

DAY 5

Chicken Livers Sauté
Brown Rice with
    Mushrooms[7]
Green Salad with Lemon
    Vinaigrette Dressing

Berry Sherbet[8]

DAY 6

Greek Lemon–Rice Soup[3]
Chicken Croquettes[3]
Spinach–Onion–Orange
    Salad[5,6]

Layered Fruit Compote[6]

DAY 7

Quick Spinach Soup[5]
Lamb Crepes Oriental[1]
Bulgur Pilaf[7]

Fresh Strawberries Plus[8]

NOTES ON SPRING MENUS

1. Buy an extra-large roast for *Leg of Lamb with Rosemary* (Day 1) so that you'll have lots left over for *Lamb Salade Niçoise* (Day 3) and *Lamb Crepes Oriental* (Day 7).
2. Leftover *Dilled New Potatoes* (Day 1) can go right into *Lamb Salade Niçoise* (Day 3). So can leftover *Asparagus Baked in Foil* (Day 1), even though the recipe doesn't call for them.
3. Make a double recipe of *Grandma's Chicken Soup* (Day 3) so that you'll have enough for *Greek Lemon–Rice Soup* (Day 6). Cook the chicken soup at least a day ahead: It's easier to degrease it after it has chilled, and you can cook chicken in it for *Chicken Hash* (Day 2) and *Chicken Croquettes* (Day 6).
4. Extra rice from *Fluffy Buttered Rice* (Day 2) can go into *Grandma's Chicken Soup* (Day 3). So can any leftover *Citrus Carrots* (Day 2).
5. Buy lots of spinach; it's used in three very different ways: *Fish Fillets with Spinach* (Day 4); *Spinach–Onion–Orange Salad* (Day 6); and *Quick Spinach Soup* (Day 7).

6. Extra bananas from *Bananas Flambé* (Day 4) and extra oranges from *Spinach–Onion–Orange Salad* (Day 6) go right into *Layered Fruit Compote* (Day 6).

7. Buy more mushrooms than you need for *Brown Rice with Mushrooms* (Day 5). Use the extras in *Bulgur Pilaf* (Day 7).

8. No need to use frozen berries in the spring when fresh strawberries are at their best. I use them twice in this week of menus, in *Berry Sherbet* (Day 5) and in *Fresh Strawberries Plus* (Day 7)—two very different, but equally delicious, desserts.

❧ SUMMER MENUS

DAY 1

Cucumber Vichyssoise

Tabouli Salad with Walnuts
Summer Squash Skillet
Pita Bread

Watermelon

DAY 2

Guacamole Salad and Corn
  Chips

Sesame Sage Chicken[1]
Rice[2]
Broiled Tomatoes with Fresh
  Herbs

Lemon Mousse

DAY 3

Manhattan Clam Chowder

Vegetable Fettuccine[3]
French Bread Glazed with
  Cheese

Mélange of Fruits

DAY 4

Cold Carrot Soup

Chicken Salad Véronique[1]
Green Salad with Vinaigrette
  Dressing

Zucchini Bread

DAY 5

Grilled Swordfish with
  Horseradish Sauce
Herbed Olive Rice[2]
Green Beans Vinaigrette

Peachy Crepes

DAY 6

Curried Caponata

Pasta Frittata[3]
Breaded Zucchini Circles

Frozen Yogurt Fruit Pie

DAY 7

Gazpacho with Yogurt

Shish Kebab
Charcoal-Broiled Vegetables
Armenian Almond–Rice Pilaf

Fresh Fruit with Toffee
  Cookies

NOTES ON SUMMER MENUS

1. Leftover chicken from *Sesame Sage Chicken* (Day 2) can be used in *Chicken Salad Véronique* (Day 4).
2. Make extra cooked *Rice* (Day 2) for *Herbed Olive Rice* (Day 5).
3. Leftover pasta from *Vegetable Fettuccine* (Day 3) is the basis for the *Pasta Frittata* (Day 6).

The main "carry-overs" in these menus are the bountiful vegetables and fruits that are the wonderful gifts of summer. Buy them at their freshest and use them in dozens of imaginative ways. Some examples follow:

Cucumbers: in *Cucumber Vichyssoise* (Day 1) and *Tahouli Salad* (Day 1).

Zucchini: in *Summer Squash Skillet* (Day 1), *Vegetable Fettuccine* (Day 3), *Zucchini Bread* (Day 4), *Breaded Zucchini Circles* (Day 6) and *Charcoal-Broiled Vegetables* (Day 7).

Tomatoes: in *Tabouli Salad* (Day 1), *Broiled Tomatoes with Fresh Herbs* (Day 2), *Manhattan Clam Chowder* (Day 3), *Herbed Olive Rice* (Day 5), *Curried Caponata* (Day 6) and *Charcoal-Broiled Vegetables* (Day 7).

Carrots: in *Tabouli Salad* (Day 1), *Manhattan Clam Chowder* (Day 3), *Vegetable Fettuccine* (Day 3) and *Cold Carrot Soup* (Day 4).

Eggplant: in *Curried Caponata* (Day 6) and *Charcoal-Broiled Vegetables* (Day 7).

Fruits: You'll need *Watermelon* (Day 1), peaches for *Peachy Crepes* (Day 5) and grapes for *Chicken Salad Véronique* (Day 4). Buy extra quantities of each of them, combine them with other fresh fruits in season (apricots, berries, etc.) and use in *Mélange of Fruits* (Day 3), *Frozen Yogurt Fruit Pie* (Day 6) and *Fresh Fruit with Toffee Cookies* (Day 7).

❧ AUTUMN MENUS

DAY 1

Stuffed Turkey Breast[1]
Pecan Sweet Potatoes
Baked Bourbon Onions with
    Mornay Sauce

Poached Apples in Citrus
    Sauce[2]

DAY 2

Mushroom Bisque[3]

Sherried Shrimp[4]
Zucchini Risotto

Filled Oatmeal Bars

DAY 3

Broiled Ham Slices with
    Fresh Pears[5]
Zucchini Salad
Pumpkin Bread

Apple Crumb Dessert[2]

DAY 4

Turkey Tetrazzini[1]
Moroccan Carrots
Spicy Beets

Spiced Pears

DAY 5

Shrimp-Stuffed Tomatoes[4]

Ham and Oyster Soup[5]
Herb Biscuits

Apple–Cranberry Frittata[2]

DAY 6

Cream of Tomato Soup

Party Pork Roast with
    Mushroom Stuffing[3]
New England Acorn Squash

Fresh Apples and Cheddar
    Cheese

DAY 7

Marinated Mushrooms[3]

Yankee Doodle Pie (with
    Ham Slices)[5]
Italian Tomato Salad

Hot Fruit Compote[2]

NOTES ON AUTUMN MENUS

1. Use leftover turkey from *Stuffed Turkey Breast* (Day 1) in *Turkey Tetrazzini* (Day 4).
2. Buy lots of apples (this is the season!) to use in *Poached Apples in Citrus Sauce* (Day 1), *Apple Crumb Dessert* (Day 3), *Apple–Cranberry Frittata* (Day 5), *Fresh Apples and Cheddar Cheese* (Day 6) and *Hot Fruit Compote* (Day 7).
3. Buy lots of mushrooms for *Mushroom Bisque* (Day 2), *Party Pork Roast with Mushroom Stuffing* (Day 6) and *Marinated Mushrooms* (Day 7).
4. Use leftover *Sherried Shrimp* (Day 2) in *Shrimp-Stuffed Tomatoes* (Day 5).
5. Allow extra ham when making *Broiled Ham Slices with Fresh Pears* (Day 3) to use in *Ham and Oyster Soup* (Day 5) and *Yankee Doodle Pie* (Day 7).

Although there's no recipe for Thanksgiving turkey in this book (we each have our own favorite recipe for this), let me call your attention to Day-After-Thanksgiving Squash (p. 127), a great way to use the leftovers from the Thanksgiving Day feast.

WINTER MENUS

DAY 1

Vegetable Soup with Basil[1]

Spaghetti with Tomato Sauce[2]
French Bread Glazed with
  Cheese

Walnut Cake with Quick
  Zabaglione Sauce

DAY 2

Herbed Roast Beef with
  Oven-Browned Potatoes[1,3]
Dilled Cucumber Salad

Frozen Mincemeat Cream

DAY 3

Greenhouse Apple Soup

Pork Chops with Hard Cider[4]
Broccoli–Cabbage Salad[5]

Cinnamon Bread Pudding

DAY 4

Cornelius's Choucroute
  Garnie[4,6]
Green Salad with Vinaigrette
  Dressing

Cheese and Fruit

DAY 5

Leftover Beef with
  Mushroom Sauce[3]
Barley Casserole
Out-of-the-Rut Rutabaga

Mocha Cream

DAY 6

Poached Eggs in Tomato
  Sauce[2]

Veal with Lemon and
  Vegetables
Rice[7]

Broiled Grapefruit with
  Amaretto

DAY 7

Broccoli Frittata[5]

Day-Before Lentil Soup with
  Sausage[6,7]
Rye Biscuits

Gingerbread with Boiled
  Cider Glaze[4]

NOTES ON WINTER MENUS

1. Cook extra potatoes in the *Vegetable Soup with Basil* (Day 1) to use in *Herbed Roast Beef with Oven-Browned Potatoes* (Day 2).

2. Make more *Homemade Tomato Sauce* than you need for the *Spaghetti* (Day 1) and use it for *Poached Eggs in Tomato Sauce* (Day 6).

3. Use leftover beef from *Herbed Roast Beef* (Day 2) in *Leftover Beef with Mushroom Sauce* (Day 5).

4. Cook extra pork chops when making *Pork Chops with Hard Cider* (Day 3) and use the leftovers in *Choucroute Garnie* (Day 4). Buy extra cider, too; you'll need it for *Gingerbread with Boiled Cider Glaze* (Day 7).

5. When making *Broccoli–Cabbage Salad* (Day 3), cook extra broccoli to use in *Broccoli Frittata* (Day 7).

6. Buy extra sausage and brown it along with the sausage for *Choucroute Garnie* (Day 4); use it in *Day-Before Lentil Soup with Sausage* (Day 7).

7. If you have any *Rice* left over from Day 6, place a spoonful on top of each serving of *Day-Before Lentil Soup* (Day 7).

❧Using Leftovers

The more I learn about cooking, the more I've come to treasure those wonderful leftovers that help me economize while providing the inspiration for other, often quite different meals. A number of the recipes in this book lend themselves easily to the use of good leftovers. For your convenience, I list them here.

USE LEFTOVER CHICKEN OR TURKEY IN:

Chicken–Walnut Pâté (p. 35)
Chicken Crepes (p. 64)
Chicken Hash (p. 65)
Chicken or Turkey Croquettes (p. 67)
Turkey Tetrazzini (p. 92)
Chicken Salad Véronique (p. 137)

USE LEFTOVER TURKEY STUFFING IN:

Day-After-Thanksgiving Squash (p. 127)

USE LEFTOVER BEEF IN:

Leftover Beef with Mushroom Sauce (p. 39)
Beef Salad Parisienne (p. 135)

USE LEFTOVER HAM IN:

Ham and Oyster Soup (p. 23)
Cornelius's Choucroute Garnie (p. 51)
Yankee Doodle Pie (p. 94)
Cheese Soufflé (p. 109)

USE LEFTOVER LAMB IN:

Lamb Crepes Oriental (p. 53)
Lamb Salade Niçoise (p. 140)

USE LEFTOVER VEGETABLES IN:

Asparagus Frittata (p. 101)
Green Beans Vinaigrette (p. 114)
Spicy Beets (p. 114)
Beet Salad (p. 135)
Broccoli Frittata (p. 100)
Corn Pancakes (p. 118)
Yorkshire Corn Pudding (p. 119)
Eggplant Frittata (p. 102)
Mushroom Bisque (p. 22)
Brown Rice with Mushrooms (p. 82)
Hot Potato Salad (p. 138)
Pumpkin Bread (p. 148)
Sausage and Potato Frittata (p. 102)
Spinach Crepes (p. 125)
Spinach Pancakes (p. 126)
Zucchini Risotto (p. 82)
Zucchini–Mushroom Quiche (p. 106)

USE LEFTOVER RICE AND PASTA IN:

Herbed Olive Rice (p. 83)
Fruited Noodle Kugel (p. 94)
Pasta Frittata (p. 101)
Rice Salad (p. 138)

USE LEFTOVER CHEESE AND EGGS IN:

Cheese Soufflé (p. 109)
Hollandaise Sauce (p. 130)
French Bread Glazed with Cheese (p. 143)
Cheese Wafers (p. 143)

USE LEFTOVER TOMATO SAUCE IN:

Poached Eggs in Tomato Sauce (p. 97)

◦❧ Index

ABOUT THE AUTHOR

CORNELIUS O'DONNELL is the spokesperson for the Consumer Products Division of Creative Services for the Corning Glass Works of Corning, N.Y. He also writes a column which currently appears in *House & Garden, Bon Appetit, Good Housekeeping, Cuisine* and *Better Homes and Gardens.* Cornelius has had a longstanding personal interest in cooking which was enhanced by working with James Beard when the dean of American cooking became a Corning representative in 1972. A native New Yorker, Cornelius was born in New York City and was raised in upstate New York. Though he travels a great deal, he makes his permanent home in Corning, New York.